Routledge Revivals

Committees

First published in 1963, Edgar Anstey's work gives a detailed account on the inner workings of the committee. Within a committee, different interests nearly always need to be represented when a decision must be taken, and contributions are required from people of different outlook or expert knowledge. A committee is often the only means of achieving a workable solution to a problem. This book attempts to analyse the functioning of different kinds of committee groups and to bring out the factors which make for efficiency and inefficiency. Types of committee and their purpose are discussed, as well as how to lead a discussion to bring out a genuine group view, the roles of chairman and secretary, how individuals influence committee decisions, good and bad tactics, and how to deal with difficult members.

Committees

How They Work and
How to Work Them

Edgar Anstey

Routledge
Taylor & Francis Group

First published in 1963
by Allen & Unwin

This edition first published in 2018 by Routledge
2 Park Square, Milton Park, Abingdon, Oxon, OX14 4RN
and by Routledge
711 Third Avenue, New York, NY 10017

Routledge is an imprint of the Taylor & Francis Group, an informa business

© 1963 Edgar Anstey

Publisher's Note
The publisher has gone to great lengths to ensure the quality of this reprint but points out that some
imperfections in the original copies may be apparent.

Disclaimer
The publisher has made every effort to trace copyright holders and welcomes correspondence from
those they have been unable to contact.
A Library of Congress record exists under ISBN: 64001251

ISBN 13: 978-1-138-55581-5 (hbk)
ISBN 13: 978-1-315-14975-2 (ebk)

Printed in the United Kingdom
by Henry Ling Limited

COMMITTEES

HOW THEY WORK
and
HOW TO WORK THEM

BY EDGAR ANSTEY

ILLUSTRATED BY THELWELL

London
GEORGE ALLEN & UNWIN LTD
RUSKIN HOUSE   MUSEUM STREET

TO MY WIFE
*in recollection of her unfailing good sense
and humour
while this book was being written*

FIRST PUBLISHED IN 1962
SECOND IMPRESSION 1963

PREFACE

The author wishes to express his gratitude to all those who have helped him in his task.

I should like to give particular thanks to Dr Sylvia Richardson of the London Institute of Education for helping me to plan the enquiries which provided material for the first draft of this book, and to Mr Cyril Martin of the Shell International Petroleum Company Ltd for his advice in rearranging a later draft. Both these friends assisted also with many detailed comments.

Thanks are due also to the following people for allowing me to seek their views on how committees work and to draw on their very wide range of experience; the positions mentioned are those held at the time that enquiries were made:

The Right Honourable The Earl Attlee, K.G., O.M., C.H.

A. H. J. Baines, Statistician, Ministry of Agriculture, Fisheries and Food

R. K. Brown, Principal, Commercial Education Department, The London Chamber of Commerce (Inc)

R. O. Clarke, Secretary, Engineering Employers London Association

G. W. M. Cockburn, Staff Administration Officer, British Broadcasting Corporation

J. Cohen, Professor of Psychology, University of Manchester

B. C. Cubbon, Principal, Cabinet Office

J. R. M. Dryden, Deputy General Secretary, The Society of Civil Servants

J. D. Handyside, Director of Research, National Institute of Industrial Psychology

F. C. Herd, Assistant Secretary, Admiralty

J. Holland, Personnel Manager, Associated TeleVision Ltd

G. Gorman, General Secretary, Friends' Service Council

Mrs M. Kohler, Clerk of a Monthly Meeting, Society of Friends

A. C. Leyton, Head of Department of Social and Industrial Studies, Northampton College of Advanced Technology, London

Miss Y. Lovat-Williams, Principal, Board of Trade

Mrs M. M. M. McArthur, Principal Psychologist, Civil Service Selection Board

Miss J. J. Nunn, Under Secretary, Home Office

A. J. Platt, O.B.E., Assistant Secretary, Treasury

Mrs P. M. Rossiter, Assistant Secretary, Treasury

J. M. Wilson, C.B., Deputy Secretary, Ministry of Aviation

In recording appreciation for the information and help received, it should be made clear that no responsibility for the opinions expressed in this book rests on the people named.

My especial thanks are given to Dr Edith Mercer, who very kindly undertook the onerous task of reading through the final draft of the book and offering detailed comments on it.

Finally, as a civil servant, I should record that, although the Ministry of Defence in which I have served during the past three years has readily agreed to my writing this book, that task has been entirely unofficial, and responsibility for the views expressed is mine alone.

NOTE ON THE AUTHOR

Dr Anstey was Head of the Civil Service Commission Research Unit from 1945-51, and from 1951-58 he was employed in the Home Office. At present he is serving in the Ministry of Defence as Senior Principal Psychologist. He has considerable experience of committee work.

CONTENTS

SCOPE OF THE BOOK

Committees have become part of our life. Large numbers of people are liable to be caught up in committee meetings from time to time. Sometimes we feel satisfied that they are both useful and mildly enjoyable. Sometimes we feel that they waste a lot of our time. This may be either because we do not seem to have much to contribute or because, when we have made some important suggestion and persuaded the committee to agree, nothing much seems to come of it anyway.

Why are some committees unsuccessful? It may be that the function of the committee is not clear, or that it overlaps with some other committee or committees. For example, at an early stage in World War II in a certain European country, two committees were set up:

(a) On steel, to seek alternative materials. It recommended wood.

(b) On wood, to seek alternative materials. It recommended steel.

There being no common membership, each committee was for a time unaware of the existence of the other. Eventually their draft reports seeped out, and both were stopped.

It may be that the committee's deliberations are of little consequence because the important decisions have already been taken elsewhere. For example, in the field of selection, a Board is sometimes summoned ostensibly to select the best from a short list of candidates: in reality the appointment has already been decided, and the Board does no more than confirm a decision already taken. To the extent that the members of the committee are aware of the position, they are likely to feel resentful that they are being used as rubber stamps.

It may be that, even when there is a definite problem to be solved, calling a committee meeting is not the best way to tackle it. It sometimes happens, for instance, that a person calls a meeting or sets up a committee when he feels tired and reluctant to continue working on his own. If the other members do not understand why they are being asked to share the responsibility for solving the problem or if they are equally tired, this achieves nothing. Success of a committee often depends on the drive and energy of the person most concerned, usually the Chairman or Secretary, who has to interest the group and make them participate. At the first meeting, for instance, of a committee newly formed in a district to give practical assistance to refugees, or of a new Sports Club committee, the first task of the convener may well be to persuade the other members that it is their responsibility to take an active part. At any committee meeting, if there are members who are just 'present' but have no desire to participate actively, then their presence is useless.

More often perhaps the committee could fulfil a useful purpose but fails to do so simply because it is run badly. Regular meetings (weekly, fortnightly or monthly) of representatives of management and staff, for instance, can help to win and retain the interest and the co-operation of staff in the work of the organization. For these committee meetings to be successful, however, the management must be prepared to take the staff into their confidence on many important issues, must be genuinely anxious to hear the staff representatives' views and to consider modifications in policy as well as in administrative detail arising from these views. If on the contrary the senior management representatives monopolize the discussion and are too freely critical of remarks by the others, the meetings will achieve little and be destructive of morale. As L. Urwick[1] put it, 'the illusion of democracy is useless'.

Recognizing these difficulties, the purpose of this book is to discuss the various kinds of committee and how they operate, and to put forward suggestions for Chairmen and members of committees which might enable them to make their committees work more efficiently.

[1] See 'Committees in Organization' in the *British Management Review* of 1937.

THE COMMITTEE SYSTEM
(as it operates in practice)

WHAT IS A COMMITTEE?

A committee is not an easy thing to define. The basic concept is a group of people sitting round a table discussing something. That much is clear. But committees differ enormously in their size, composition, frequency of meetings, how they were set up, in their purpose and objectives, and in their rules (or absence of rules) of procedure. It is often difficult to say, for instance, exactly how and when a series of meetings that started as a casual get-together between a few people turned into a committee; or to draw the line between a committee meeting and a conference. Yet some definition of a committee must be attempted in order to indicate the sort of meetings that are or are not covered by this book.

Professor W. J. M. Mackenzie[1] has defined a committee as 'A body of people meeting round a table, to take decisions for joint action on behalf of some other (generally larger) body of which it is the committee'. The committee thus has a common purpose, and some kind of a constitution. It follows rules, though it may have made some of the rules itself. It contains more than two people and becomes unwieldy if it has more than twenty-five. Mackenzie points out that the Cabinet in relation to the majority of the House of Commons is both master and servant—so are all committees. A committee must reach decisions, even if they are all subject to confirmation by its parent body. It must say: 'These points are clear: accept them, give us directives on the others'. Mackenzie's definition has two defects. It makes no mention of any terms of reference, but every committee must be constrained by some limitation on the subjects for

[1] See 'Committees in Administration' in *Public Administration*, Autumn 1953.

consideration, or its discussion would be endless. And it places too great an emphasis on the mere taking of decisions to the neglect of the discussion and free exchange of views which are part of the *raison d'être* of any true committee.

COLLECTIVE RESPONSIBILITY

Also implicit in the concept of a committee is the doctrine of collective responsibility. By this is meant that after there has been full and free discussion of a matter, a group decision is reached which is regarded as a shared decision to be accepted loyally by all. Each member of the committee is then prepared (whatever personal reservations he may feel) to support the group decision and any action arising from it against possible attack from outside the group. If the committee does well, each member can take credit for its success. If it makes a mistake, the blame attached to any one member is reduced by being shared with the rest.

It may be of interest to digress for a few moments and note the rather different emphasis placed on collective responsibility in the USA and in Britain. In the UK this doctrine is stressed in all committees from the highest to the lowest. The emphasis on collective responsibility for Cabinet decisions derives from the responsibility of the Executive to Parliament, and is explained in the ancient saying 'If we don't hang together, we shall all be hanged separately'. In the USA, where under the constitution the Executive is not responsible to Congress, the tradition of collective responsibility is less strong. In matters of government the Americans are more inclined, by history and by temperament, to look for decisions by a leader, when the British would look for decisions by a group of people. An example of working methods that would seem strange to any Englishman but might seem less strange to an American is provided by the following extract from *Russia and the West under Lenin and Stalin* by George F. Kennan. Referring to the decision in July 1918 to send an expeditionary force to Siberia, Kennan writes: 'Wilson had taken this decision, as was his habit, in complete loneliness and privacy. He was a man who was not given to consulting with anyone, and particularly anyone not under his own authority.' This different stress on collective responsibility at governmental level makes a British Cabinet less tolerant of blunders than an American Cabinet would be, since, so long as the Minister who had blundered remained in the Government, all his colleagues would have to share responsibility for his mistake. For example when Sir Samuel Hoare misjudged the temper of the British people by subscribing to the Hoare-Laval proposals regarding Abyssinia in 1935, he was disowned by his colleagues and resigned the post of Foreign Secretary. (This did not prevent him from returning to the Cabinet, after a decent interval, as First Lord of the Admiralty in 1936.) An American Cabinet Minister who had made a similar error might have found it possible to remain in the government, since, if he did so, his colleagues might still not have felt it necessary to share responsibility for his mistake.

This is not to suggest that there is less extensive use of committees in the USA than in Britain, but merely that the outlook is somewhat different. It has been said that the three great democracies of France, Britain and the USA all believe in liberty, equality and fraternity. But whereas in France the greatest emphasis is on equality, in Britain it is on liberty, and in the USA on fraternity. Members of an American committee may feel all buddies together and yet believe that they need an undisputed leader. Members of a corresponding British committee may feel distinct reservations towards each other socially and yet believe that each member is entitled to voice his personal views before the group view is formed. An advantage of the American outlook is that decisions can be reached more quickly, with an obvious gain in efficiency. An advantage of the British outlook is that a decision once reached is less likely to be queried later by any member of the committee or to be reversed on a change of Chairman.

The definition of a committee used in this book is as follows:
'A group of people appointed by some other, generally larger, body (or bodies) to meet and discuss matters within some field of reference, with a view to making group decisions or recommendations to the parent body (or bodies).'

Some thoughts included in the above definition are:

(1) The committee has a definite composition.

(2) It is set up by, and is in some sense ultimately responsible to, a parent body (or bodies).

(3) The ultimate purpose is to take group decisions, but these may be either final decisions or mere recommendations.

(4) The taking of decisions is preceded by a discussion and exchange of views sufficient to ensure that the decision is a decision of the whole group (or, in certain instances perhaps, of a majority of the group, with the minority opinion also recorded).

One sort of situation in which a committee as defined above is likely to be useful is when interests conflict among people of equal status. The person responsible for resolving the conflict may then consider that it would help him to make the best decision if he could have a comprehensive and reasoned presentation of the arguments for and against possible courses of action, and that such a presentation could best be provided by a committee of the interested parties.

It will be seen that the definition does not stipulate a Chairman. A committee usually has an acknowledged Chairman, but this is not absolutely essential. For example, the Chairmanship can rotate between different members. Nor does the definition stipulate that the committee records its views in a written minute or report. This is almost invariably the case, but there may be certain committees which report orally to their parent bodies and should still be regarded as committees. The definition does, however, exclude large gatherings of people held solely in order to exchange information and views and not in order to reach group decisions or tender advice.

All committees included within the above definition will have much in common; they will be groups of people discussing something and trying to reach a measure of agreement. Most of what follows in this book, therefore, will be general advice applicable to all kinds of committee. Certain matters, however, for example, the optimum number of members, will be dependent on the type of committee in mind, for which reason a general classification of committees may be helpful.

CLASSIFICATION OF COMMITTEES

Committees can be classified according to their time scale. purpose, and composition:

Time Scale

(1) A Standing Committee, which meets at intervals (often regular intervals) over an indefinite period of time and considers a variety of problems as they become important.

(2) An *Ad hoc* Committee—often known as a Working Party—appointed to study a particular problem. Its job done, such a committee is expected to dissolve.

Purpose

(1) An Executive Committee, which has power to take final decisions and enforce them. Examples are the Board of a private business or nationalized industry, or the Executive of a sports club. Unless its decisions seem likely to be questioned, an Executive Committee does not normally have to prepare a full report in explanation of them.

(2) An Advisory Committee, whose main purpose is the tendering of advice or the airing of views, which may or may not be accepted, e.g. the committees of Town, Borough or District Councils. An Advisory Committee has normally to prepare a persuasive report.

The P.E.P. book on *Advisory Committees in British Government*[1] lists some 480 such committees, mainly with mixed voluntary (non-official) and official membership though some contain non-officials only. Some examples

[1] Allen & Unwin.

A *Homogeneous Committee*

taken at random, are the Consultative Committee for Industry, which is concerned with Britain's overseas trade; the Central Housing Advisory Committee, with numerous sub-committees on various aspects of housing; the Committee on Road Safety; and the Advisory Council on the Treatment of Offenders.

Composition

(1) Homogeneous, i.e. people from a common background, or with similar jobs, or showing a common interest. Examples would be the Executive Committee of an Old School association; a committee of representative Establishment Officers, or Personnel Managers from a related group of industrial firms; or the committee of a literary, artistic or social society.

(2) Joint, i.e. representing two contrasting interests, which may be expected to negotiate with each other. There may be representatives, e.g. of management and staff; of Conservatives and Labour; of a government department and a local authority; of doctors and administrators; or of scien-

tists and military personnel. Such a committee may have 8-20 members.

(3) Mixed, representing a variety of different points of view. Some members may, for example, be experts and others laymen; some may be voluntary workers and others paid officials. Such a committee may well be large, with twenty or more members, some of whom will have only limited information about the matters discussed.

Mixed committees can be subdivided into two classes according to the responsibility of members:

(a) Representative. Each member is a delegate from some organisation and on some points will not be able to vary his views without reference back to that organisation.

(b) Personal. The views that each member expresses are purely personal, and he can vary them without reference back to anybody.

The distinction between voluntary (unpaid) and official membership is important as regards selection of committee members, and these two classes of members will be considered separately in chapter 3. Apart from the selection aspect, however, this distinction is not so important as to warrant complicating the classification with additional subheadings, especially as many committees, e.g. the Executive Committees of some Trade Unions and Voluntary Organizations, have mixed voluntary and official membership.

Committees vary in the frequency with which they meet. Standing Committees meet usually at regular intervals, (say) monthly or quarterly. If the meetings are irregular and the convener of a meeting waits for what he considers to be an adequate volume of business to accumulate (for instance, the notice displayed in a certain canteen that 'The Committee will meet as and when the Chairman decides') there is danger that some items will fail to receive reasonably prompt attention and that the committee will gradually fall into decay. Ad hoc Committees usually have a fairly rapid succession of meetings until their particular task has been accomplished.

Committees vary also in their working methods, as will

be described in chapter 4. Their methods are, however, largely within their own discretion and are not inherent in the committee as set up. Method is not therefore an appropriate basis for initial classification.

3

COMPOSITION OF COMMITTEES

OPTIMUM SIZE

Committees vary considerably in size, and the best size will depend on the nature and purpose of the particular committee. One advantage of a small committee is that each member has more chance to speak and to ensure that group decisions are implemented to his satisfaction. From the point of view of firm, consistent, speedy executive action, it has often been said that the ideal committee is a committee of one. Indeed a certain American experiment, in which the degree of satisfaction felt by members of various committees was plotted against the number of members, found that the curve of satisfaction rose steadily as the numbers decreased, continued to rise even as the number of members was reduced from 2 to 1, and reached a theoretical maximum at about 0·7. This argument of course has its dangers. It may be tempting, for instance, for the captain of a sports club to run its affairs dictatorially, with only a minimum of consultation from time to time with other members of a committee that never meets. If he is palpably efficient and well liked by most members of the club, he may succeed in getting away with this for several years. In due course, however, sufficient members will have become resentful of the captain's high-handed conduct to insist on the club being organized on more democratic lines.

One advantage of a relatively large committee is that more interests can be represented on it and there can be greater exchange of information and views. On the other hand, a larger membership makes it more difficult to arrange meetings to suit the convenience of all members, and to allow anyone who wishes to speak at a meeting to do so without the meeting becoming excessively long. The meetings of very large committees with 40 or more members, e.g. the Councils of certain learned societies, are often dreadfully tedious and inefficient. Attendance tends to be irregular, and often members do not know each other. This is clearly shown by the fact that, when a new member appears, some old members do not know whether he is new or not. Many members, when they do turn up at meetings, pay scant attention to what is going on. In such circumstances it is impossible for the committee to develop a proper corporate spirit. It would be much better if the permanent members were reduced in number to 20 or fewer people, all willing and able to attend meetings regularly, on the understanding that additional members could be co-opted for particular meetings as and when the need arose.

Another reason for not increasing the membership above 18-20 is that above this level there is an overwhelming tendency for one or more smaller sub-committees to form, officially or unofficially. These inner groups keep all the power in their hands, so that other members of the committee become superfluous. There is some evidence to show[1] that in a large unstructured committee with N members, most of whom vote randomly, a 'cell' with $\sqrt{N}$ members all voting consistently together can dominate the committee proceedings completely. For example, in a Trade Union committee with 25 members, a group of 5 or more extremists of some kind might be able to control the whole committee if there were no organized opposition to them. If the committee has fewer members, there is less tendency or opportunity for this to happen without being noticed.

For committees which are 'joint' or 'mixed' in composition, a membership of 9-11 may be about right. If the committee is smaller than that, the absence from a particular meeting of one member, especially if he has expert knowledge, may unbalance the committee. For the committee to contain a few 'passengers', i.e. less energetic and talkative members, may be an advantage. Such persons are likely to hold a middle view and to be amenable to persuasion by whoever presents the best arguments. This lessens the risk of deadlock between two strongly opposing views which might take place, e.g. in a committee of only 6 members.

[1] See article by L. S. Penrose in the *Journal* of the Royal Statistical Society 1946, Vol. 109.

A *Mixed Committee* (see pages 18-19)

For committees which are homogeneous in composition, an adequate balance of opinion may well be secured by a smaller number of members, (say) 5 or 7.

REASONS WHY PEOPLE COME ON COMMITTEES

People are normally chosen to serve on business committees either by virtue of the position that they hold, e.g. Personnel Manager, or because they are regarded as particularly suitable to serve on the committee.

People do not normally serve on voluntary committees unless they have volunteered or at least signified willingness to do so. Among the reasons why people are willing to serve on committees without payment are:

(a) Keen interest in the subject matter and a desire to correct abuses or devise reforms;

(b) Family tradition;

(c) Sense of duty;

(d) Sociability and desire to conform, if one's friends are already serving on the committee and invite one to join them on it;

(e) Desire to fill in time and make oneself useful. This is most likely for retired people and middle-aged housewives, who find that they have more time on their hands than they used to have.

On rare occasions, the dominating motive may be self-interest. In one case reported to the author, a man sought election to the local Parish Council because he wanted a street lamp erected outside his gate. When this lamp had been erected, he promptly resigned from the Council. More frequently, while other motives are dominant, a candidate for the local Council may not be wholly uninfluenced by the hope that, if elected, he may be able to do his family or his friends a bit of good. It is only fair to add that, if such motives are in fact put into effect and become apparent, the Councillor usually fails to secure re-election.

Whatever other reasons he may have for wishing to join a Committee, a motive that is certain to be present to a lesser or greater extent is desire for increased power, influence and prestige. Were it not for this motive, very few voluntary committees would be fully manned. Up to a point this motive may be beneficial. The desire for recognition as a good committee member is likely to prompt a person to be more alert, interested and energetic than he would be otherwise, and quite modest success and recognition may suffice to keep him content. The danger comes when the desire for power becomes the dominant motive. The need grows with what it feeds on until nothing less than steadily increasing recognition and power will satisfy the person concerned. He will no longer be content to be an ordinary committee member, but will expect to become Chairman or at least to be acknowledged as a specially valuable and important member, to be consulted as a matter of course on all points. Often such persons get on more committees than they can cope with. Their judgment thus becomes less and less valuable, while they still retain disproportionate influence and prestige. A person who obtains a powerful position in this way may succeed in dominating the committee when he is present, but it is interesting to note that when he is not present his views, if known, are usually voted against: this shows the latent antagonism of other members of the group.

Some people, on the other hand, with no craving for power, become inveigled into joining several committees through a combination of sense of duty and inability to say No. They find themselves drawn into a seemingly endless round of meetings, in much the same way that other people become entangled in hire purchase repayments. No sooner has one committee finished its work than they become involved in another. For meetings to seem a burden rather than a pleasure should be taken by the person concerned as a warning signal that he has perhaps joined too many committees and should take stock of the position, concentrating on those in which he is really interested and seeking an opportunity to retire gracefully from any others. Like all good resolutions, however, this may be more easily taken than carried out.

SELECTION OF COMMITTEE MEMBERS

Any member of a committee should be able to contribute some relevant knowledge or experience to its deliberations. An equally desirable qualification is willingness to listen quietly and, on occasions, to admit ignorance of the matter being discussed. To take a trivial but all too common example, whenever an 'expert' is holding forth and using either technical jargon or a string of initials, a useful function is performed by the committee member who has the courage to admit that he does not know what is meant by (say) a 'Sunshine Unit'[1] or a F.P.S.M.G.[2] and to request an explanation.

The principle that members of the committee should be representative of all points of view is a good principle which is sometimes carried too far, with the result that the committee becomes too large. It is not necessary for every con-

[1] One micro-micro-curie of Strontium 90 per gram of Calcium.
[2] Farm Price Support Major Granary.

ceivable interest to be represented on the committee, so long as there is provision for all relevant points of view to become known, either orally or in writing. Even on a 'joint' committee, there is advantage in having some members who represent no particular interest and have no axes to grind.

Excessively shy or excessively domineering people are to be avoided. With this single reservation, almost any other type of person is capable of becoming a useful committee member. Under skilful Chairmanship, it is to be expected that the members of any committee will quickly get to know each other and work happily together. More often than not, the various members develop a keen corporate sense and strong feelings of loyalty to the group.

Indeed, there is a real danger that the group loyalties may in time become excessive and to some extent blind the committee members to the true opinions and feelings of the people they are supposed to represent. An interesting example of this was when a local Councillor who had given good service for six years moved to an adjoining ward. At the next election he was unanimously recommended for re-nomination by the 48 members of the Residents' Association committee, all of whom knew him well. This decision, however, roused a storm of protest from other residents, who took the view that he could no longer represent the local interest while living in another ward, since the interests of the two wards might quite likely conflict. An Extraordinary General Meeting of the Association had to be summoned, at which another resident, newly arrived in the district and not on the committee, was chosen as the Association's candidate in preference to the retiring Councillor.

SELECTION OF THE CHAIRMAN

The Chairman usually plays a key rôle (see chapter 6), and the selection of a suitable Chairman is of particular importance. It might be thought that the choice should naturally fall on the most impressive, experienced and influential member of the committee. Curiously enough, this view cannot be advanced without two reservations. First it may prove a disadvantage if the Chairman is so eminent and expert that other members are overawed and unduly deferent to his opinion. It might sometimes be preferable for the Chairman to be a less senior person, not specially expert technically, and not particularly imposing in appearance, provided of course that he is able to keep control. Second and more important, it is to be expected that a person who has occupied a position of great personal responsibility and authority and who is used to making decisions without first taking advice from colleagues (such as a judge perhaps, or the owner of a newspaper) might find it difficult to act as Chairman of a committee. Some such people might be able to adapt themselves to the very different situation, but others, with the best will in the world, might find the task impossible.

The ideal Chairman is someone who on the one hand commands the respect of his committee, but who on the other hand is not completely reliant on his own judgment and is ready and accustomed to take the general feeling of the group. He should know enough about committee procedure not to be hidebound by it but to be able to interpret points of order so as to keep the proceedings running smoothly. While concerned that the committee should act sensibly, he should not feel that his personal prestige depends upon particular decisions made by the committee. The basic requirement for the Chairman is that he should inspire confidence, so that all members of the committee trust him.

4

COMMITTEE METHODS

While the methods used by different committees vary widely in detail, basically they fall into one or other of two groups. These depend on whether the discipline governing the behaviour of members at committee meetings is in the main external or internal.

At meetings governed in the main by an external discipline, the contributions that any individual member can make are limited by set rules enshrined in the constitution or established by the practice of the committee, and interpreted and applied by the Chairman. The rules are designed to facilitate keeping order and to enable sensible decisions to be reached quickly and with least effort. The Chairman has authority to ensure that preference is given to those members who can make the most useful contributions, so that committee time is occupied as efficiently as possible. At meetings of this type, the proceedings are usually formal, with precise agenda and a limited amount of time for discussing each item. Any member wishing to speak must catch the Chairman's eye, and it is within the discretion of the Chairman to select the next speaker and to decide when discussion of any item has gone on long enough and any disagreements must be resolved by majority vote. The theory underlying this method of committee meeting is that, even when all the relevant facts have been made known, opinions are liable to differ; that it is not therefore always possible for the committee to reach agreement and prolonging the discussion indefinitely serves no useful purpose; and that after a reasonable amount of time has been allowed for discussion and exchange of views, the best course is to sound the opinion of the meeting (either by a formal vote or by some other device) and then go on to the next item on the agenda. The Chairman controls the proceedings so as to achieve precise objectives.

At meetings governed in the main by an internal discipline, there are few rules governing procedure. Any individual member is free to speak at any time and, within reason, for as long as he wishes. To avert clashes between different members wishing to speak at once and to prevent the meetings from being excessively lengthy, the main reliance is on the self-restraint of each member, which prevents him from addressing the meeting except when he is convinced that he has a worthwhile contribution to make towards the group objective of arriving at the best conclusion. Discussions at this type of meeting are free and liable to be discursive. The Chairman has less authority (sometimes no authority) either to select the next speaker or to terminate discussion of any item except with the unanimous agreement of the meeting. His main function is to make sure that all contributions are understood aright by other members of the committee, to guide the meeting as necessary with this objective in mind, and to interpret the general opinion of the meeting when he feels that agreement has been reached. The theory underlying this method of committee meeting is that, provided all the relevant facts have been made known and all members who wished to speak have been enabled to do so, it should be possible for unanimous agreement to be reached; but that on difficult issues this agreement may take a long time to reach and that nothing is gained by cutting the discussion short and taking a majority vote.

This division of committees according to method cuts right across the classification of committees described in chapter 2. It is not whether the committee is Standing or Ad hoc, Executive or Advisory, which determines its method of operation, but the general belief of its members on how its business can best be conducted. Size is relevant, however. The smaller the committee, the easier it should be for it to operate by free discussion. The larger the committee, the greater is likely to be the pressure for external rules to help the Chairman to keep order and get through the business in a reasonable time. A measure of external discipline would seem inevitable if most of the members represent narrow interests and only the Chairman can take a broad view.

Joint committees require special mention, since it might be thought that they must necessarily operate within special constraints. Taking joint consultation committees in industry, for example, it might seem desirable that successive speakers should normally come alternately from the management and staff sides, and inevitable that all members from the same side should follow the same general line. Experience suggests, however, that the less strictly members of a joint consultation committee feel obliged to abide by these restrictions, the more useful the committee will become. An interesting article by F. Fuerstenberg entitled 'Dynamics of Joint Consultation' appeared in the September 1959 issue of the *British Journal of Sociology*. In this article Fuerstenberg reviewed the background of joint consultation in a particular nationalized industry with 40 local committees, and discussed the work of one joint consultation committee studied over a period of four years. He found that:

(1) With increasing experience the attitudes of committee members became somewhat more flexible during this period and the distinction between management and staff points of view became less clear cut.

(2) Managers were required to use negotiating skill at these meetings.

(3) 'Wholehearted agreement is only possible on the basis of the right to disagree, as true co-operation can only be obtained from people who are free to refuse it.' The chief value of joint consultation committees is that decisions reached in this way are likely to carry greater authority and to be accepted more widely and wholeheartedly than decisions made by management without recourse to joint consultation.

CONVENTIONAL COMMITTEE METHODS

Examples of committees which use the first method are local authority Councils, and Resident Association committees; and of those which use the second method informal *ad hoc* business committees, Inter-Services study groups and

Quakers. Features of the first method are that it assumes:
(1) That, for practical purposes, the majority is always right.
(2) That at committee meetings the majority vote will represent the majority opinion.
(3) That the outvoted minority will acquiesce in the majority ruling.

Each of these assumptions, though normally reasonable, proves false on occasion. Assumption (1), for example, may not be justified when there is an apparent conflict between local and broader interests; then the majority of members of a local committee, unless they are extraordinarily far-sighted people, may take a parochial view of the matter. In the case of the current proposals for the reorganization of local government in the Greater London area, for instance, nearly every local authority council concerned has voted against acceptance of the scheme. Yet (without prejudging the merits or demerits of these proposals) the scheme was conceived in the interests of all, and the Government's view is that it would on balance be beneficial to all. Certainly, to take a more obvious historical example, the general fears that the introduction of the spinning jenny would lead to widespread unemployment in the cotton industry did not prove justified in the event.

An occasion when assumption (2) might not be justified would be when one influential member of a committee has made a persuasive speech, particularly if it was emotional in tone and contained an appeal for group solidarity and loyalty—as might happen, for instance, at a meeting of a strike committee. The other members would then be reluctant to vote against such an appeal, even though they might privately incline to follow a different course.

Difficulties arise over assumption (3) when a slight nuisance to the majority has to be balanced against a considerable boon to a few. For example, when a certain model aeroplane club was trying to find a suitable piece of level ground on which to fly its planes, every suggested site was opposed by residents in the neighbourhood on the grounds that the noise of the model planes would be a nuisance to them. The local council more than once voted by a small majority against granting facilities in the district, but the outvoted minority refused to admit that the club's claims had been considered properly and persisted in pressing the matter until eventually a suitable site was found.

Features of the second method are that it assumes:

(1) That there is a solution to any human problem which is the 'best' solution that can be reached in the circumstances.

(2) That any group of human beings should be sufficiently reasonable to recognize and accept this best solution after full discussion.

(3) That a full discussion will not take an intolerably long time.

Each of these assumptions also is questionable, but the method can be illustrated by describing a typical monthly meeting of the Society of Friends, who believe strongly in, and practise, this informal approach.

THE QUAKER APPROACH

The meeting began with half an hour of prayer in silence broken only by the Clerk drawing attention, after about 15 minutes, to the recent death of a Friend and by observations by one of the Elders. This silent prayer seemed to have the effect of bringing those present into a humble frame of mind and of fostering general goodwill and desire to co-operate for the common good.

The practice, after each item has been dealt with, is for the Clerk to read out a minute, which he has drafted on the spot, and to seek general endorsement of it. The Clerk did this with ease and in most cases (though not all) there was immediate general agreement. This practice avoids argument and possible recriminations at a later date about what was resolved at the time.

There was particularly interesting discussion of an item on which obviously there has been considerable differences of opinion, namely the proposal to split the monthly meeting, which covered a large area, known as 'Dewhurst, Laxton and Midchester', into two smaller areas. The previous monthly meeting had agreed that the division should be made and the boundary had been settled, but it had been left to this monthly meeting to propose (for endorsement by the superior regional meeting) names for the two new areas.

As soon as this item was introduced by the Clerk, an animated discussion followed, and several suggestions were put forward for naming the new areas. These suggestions included, for the western area, 'Midchester and Ripworth', 'Midchester', and 'West Loamshire', and for the eastern area, 'Dewhurst and Laxton', 'Dewhurst, Laxton and East-bury', and 'East Loamshire'. Each speaker gave cogent reasons why his or her own suggestion was a sensible one for historical, geographical or practical reasons, and why the other suggestions were less satisfactory. That even Friends are human in finding it difficult completely to abandon previous opinions was shown by one speaker remarking that 'At the last meeting we were guided or misguided to agree to splitting the monthly meeting . . . ' Apart perhaps from this faint indication of lingering discontent, the discussion was amicable but in view of the diversity of opinion prospects of agreement seemed poor. The Clerk was moved to suggest that, if members found it difficult to agree, a decision on the titles had better be postponed to the next meeting; meanwhile Friends could think about the matter further. Whether this suggestion was intended to be taken literally or whether it was a subtle way of reminding the members of the desirability of reaching agreement was not clear. Anyway the effect, after a pause during which no one spoke but everyone doubtless reflected that the question of titles was after all a secondary one and that it should be possible for all present to agree, was remarkable. After two or three minutes, one Friend suggested that the titles 'Midchester' and 'Dewhurst and Laxton' seemed the simplest ones, involving least departure from the present name for the combined area. Another member pointed out that not to mention other towns, e.g. Ripworth, in the first title did not imply that those towns were of lesser importance. It would be cumbersome to include several towns in the title, and so there was a lot to be said for naming only the largest towns. Other members quickly signified their assent by nodding or saying 'I agree', and this suggestion was carried unanimously, with obvious pleasure all round that a satisfactory decision had been reached.

The discussion of this item seemed to me to reveal three points which would be worth bearing in mind when considering committees generally.

(a) While Quakers are helped by knowledge of a common faith, customs and interest and by feelings of group solidarity, they do not necessarily find it easier than the next man to agree quickly on a difficult point.

(b) When apparent deadlock is reached, reiteration of the arguments on either side is useless. There is great advantage in the technique by which the Clerk calls for a pause for reflection before anyone else speaks. This allows each person time to reflect on the possible merits of other suggestions and to consider whether he really wishes to press his own view any further. [Without a fundamental reservoir of goodwill, the technique would not necessarily work, since obstinate members of a group might use the pause to think up fresh arguments in support of their own point of view. On balance, however, a pause must almost always be helpful.]

(c) In such a situation, what is required is either some sort of compromise or, better still where circumstances permit, a fresh suggestion, possibly something quite different from those already discussed. The chance of a member being inspired to put forward a fresh suggestion is greatly increased by a silent pause for reflection.

A striking contrast with the atmosphere described in this account of a Quaker meeting is provided in the accounts of committee meetings and the negotiations leading up to them in novels by C. P. Snow such as *The Masters* and *The Affair*. The characters in these novels differ in other respects but most of them seem obsessed with power politics. They form violently partisan views on some matter of common concern, such as the election of a new Master, and spare no effort in striving to achieve the result they desire. The assumptions on which they seem to act, though these are taken for granted rather than stated explicitly, are:

(*a*) That on important issues such as the election of a new Master there are bound to be contending interests which make general agreement impossible.

(*b*) That, if the exponents of the opposite point of view cannot be squared, they must be opposed ruthlessly to the end. Some of the characters are more squeamish than others about the methods used, but each is prepared to devote his full intellect and will towards gaining the result he wants.

(*c*) That, if the decision they seek seems likely to have a disastrous effect on certain colleagues who take the opposite view, this effect, though unfortunate, is inevitable and is certainly not their fault. C. P. Snow's books are of absorbing interest. People like his characters no doubt exist in real life, but it is as well that there are not too many of them. Otherwise the world would be a much less pleasant place to live in than in fact it is.

The Quaker view that their method is best for them rests on the belief that each individual Friend, if he puts his trust in God, as revealed through his own conscience and the utterances of other Friends, will be guided to the truth. While non-Quakers would not necessarily share this particular belief, they might agree that the method of trying to thrash a matter out until general agreement is reached often offers a better chance of achieving a satisfactory and lasting solution than does the method of deciding by majority vote after a more limited period of discussion.

CONDITIONS FOR A SATISFACTORY COMMITTEE

There are many committees for which some combination of the two methods would seem desirable. If the meeting is run on formal lines, it is still desirable that the feeling of the whole meeting should be sought actively. Not only should any member who has anything worthwhile to offer be encouraged to speak, but there should also be widespread sharing among committee members of any tasks consequent upon the discussion, e.g. checking some background information, drafting, etc. If the meeting is run on informal lines, it will still be necessary for the Chairman to control manifest irrelevancies and to bring the meeting back to the item under discussion as need arises.

A difficult situation arises when, even after a full discussion and the most thorough explanation of why people think as they do, one or more members of the committee find that they still dissent from the major view. It may then be difficult for a dissenting member to decide whether he should continue to hold out against his colleagues or acquiesce in the majority view. If he is a delegate to a 'Representative' committee, the Chairman may have to ask him to go away and seek fresh instructions. If his views are purely personal, the Chairman should seek to persuade him to fall in with the majority. The dissentient should stand firm, however, on points of 'principle or conscience'. Any group of people working together over a period will almost inevitably develop a corporate spirit and desire to conform. Tolerance of differences of opinion within the group is equally desirable and important.

Whatever the methods used, a satisfactory committee should satisfy certain conditions:

(1) It should be clear as to its purpose and powers.

(2) It should be able to understand, discuss and criticize any proposals put before it, and not just act as a rubber stamp.

(3) It should reach decisions as a group, and not be dominated by any one member.

(4) It should be able to express its policy and decisions to people outside the committee in such a way that they genuinely represent the group opinion.

RESEARCH INTO COMMITTEE METHODS

Some aspects at least of the different methods used by different committees should be subject to controlled experiment, with a view to determining which methods help to make the committees most efficient. Having said this much, however, it must be stressed that results from any one experiment are not necessarily applicable to committees which are not similar in character to those studied in the experiment.

One interesting experiment was reported in chapter 3 of *Groups, Leadership and Men*, edited by Harold Guetzkow (Carnegie Press, 1951). The chapter was entitled 'A Social Psychology Study of the Decision-making Conference'. It described a field study made of 72 committees from various organizations, each with 5-17 members all of whom had previously worked together. Four observers noted each meeting, recording, for example, how much each member participated, how often he said 'I' or 'We' and how satisfied he seemed with a group decision. There was reasonable agreement between ratings by different observers (the average correlation coefficient being about 0·7), suggesting that the observations were fairly reliable.

Three separate criteria were studied, namely Satisfaction of members with the meeting, Productivity of the group, and Amount of residual disagreement after the meeting, and it was found that:

(1) Members tended to feel more satisfaction if the group had a definite structure and followed formal rules of procedure, and if members did not feel that they had to assert themselves unduly in order to receive a fair hearing.[1] Whether members participated to an equal extent did not affect their degree of satisfaction, so long as each member felt that he had the *opportunity* to say what he wanted.

(2) Groups tended to get through more items of business if they felt that the problems discussed were urgent, if they knew that they had authority to deal with these problems themselves, and if they tackled them in an orderly and systematic manner.

(3) Residual disagreement was greater when there were differences of opinion as to goals, when individual members felt that their prestige demanded that their own points of view be accepted,[1] and if there was a feeling of inadequate power to deal with the problems discussed.

[1] Each of these is a free translation to suit the particular context. The author apologizes if he has not caught the correct meaning of the original phrase, which was the display of a greater or lesser amount of 'self-oriented need behaviour'.

(4) Though each of these criteria had some relevance, no two of them correlated highly with each other, and no single criterion or any combination of them provided an adequate measure of the success or efficiency of a meeting.

The relative importance of the three criteria would probably differ in different circumstances. For example, when dealing with a series of relatively superficial items, formality of procedure would make for speed and satisfaction, which in this case would be true measures of efficiency. When dealing with a single profound problem, however, it is possible that a more informal approach, of the kind discussed earlier in this chapter, might be more likely to lead eventually to a generally acceptable and lasting solution. The index of 'Productivity' for such a meeting might be low, but this would be irrelevant in the particular context. The conclusions from Guetzkow's field study are not therefore very important in this context, but the study was useful in pointing the way to further research which should be undertaken in this field.

Committees are highly individual, and any generalizations about them should be made with great care. Nevertheless the helpfulness or otherwise of various kinds of procedure could well be tested by scientific experiment. For example, secret ballot voting procedures could be tried out, as a possible means of preventing a committee from being dominated by one member with a very powerful personality, particularly if this member happens to be the Chairman.

Another possible line of study would be to provide each member of a committee with a chess-clock (a device similar to the kitchen 'timer') to be set in motion whenever he was speaking and at each meeting allow him a definite ration of time for speaking. Thus if the Committee had 2 hours available for a meeting and 5 members, it might seem reasonable to allow each member up to 20 minutes, with an extra 20 minutes for the Chairman. Each member could use his ration of time as he wished, in one lengthy speech or in a series of brief interjections, so long as he did not exceed a total of 20 minutes.

5

TRAINING IN COMMITTEE WORK

THREE KINDS OF PRACTICE COMMITTEE MEETING

Considering the frequency and importance of committee meetings, it is remarkable how little attention appears to have been given to training in this subject. Quite a number of organizations give instruction in the purely formal aspects of committee work, e.g. on committee procedure (including the formal duties of a Chairman), on drafting reports, and on the duties of a committee secretary. Advice on these formal aspects is set out in pamphlets such as *Committee Procedure* issued by the Treasury for official use in 1958, *Notes for the Guidance of Committee Secretaries* issued by the Home Office for official use also in 1958, and *The ABC of Chairmanship* by Lord Citrine, all admirable of their kind but limited in scope. The written pamphlets are illustrated and supplemented, in many organizations, by practical demonstrations and courses. As a rule, however, neither the pamphlets nor the courses deal effectively with the handling of people or give adequate advice on human problems or on preventing such problems arising or becoming acute. An exception to this general statement is the excellent pamphlet *Conference Leading* published in 1959 by the National Institute for Industrial Psychology, who also are concerned with human problems in many of their courses. Apart from the NIIP, there are very few organizations which provide systematic instruction specifically in how to handle people at committee meetings. This is surprising, because to give training in committee work is not a particularly difficult thing to do. Practice committee meetings can easily be made interesting, stimulating and enjoyable. No special equipment or apparatus is required. A tape recorder is useful but not indispensable. The only essential requirements are that the trainees should be responsive and willing to learn, and that the training officer should have a clear idea of what he is after and should be alert to pick out relevant examples of interesting committee behaviour as they occur.

If one wishes to organize practice committee meetings, the first thing to decide is the kind of subject to be discussed. There are three possibilities:

(1) A topic from current affairs on which the trainees can be invited to give their real opinions. If they are to start on reasonably equal terms, this must be a topic of general interest such as capital punishment, the effects of television, or reform of the licensing laws. A topic of this kind has the advantages of needing little preparation by the training officer and of allowing the trainees to speak naturally and not act parts. The discussion is, however, likely to resemble a debate rather than a committee meeting of the kind that the trainees are likely to meet in their jobs. Nor, in view of their varying interests in current affairs, can they start on completely equal terms when discussing any such topic.

(2) The second method is to use a wholly invented topic set out in a dossier of papers prepared beforehand by the training officer. Topics of this kind have been prepared regularly by the Civil Service Selection Board in a series of 'background stories'. Each background story file gives a full account of an imaginary island, or similar close-knit community, with all the relevant facts about it, and presents a series of problems for discussion. If the group contains (say) 7 candidates, then 7 problems are discussed one after another, each candidate taking his turn to act as Chairman. As an example of the sort of problem presented, the group might be asked to imagine that the sum of £500,000 had been donated to the island Government and to discuss various ways in which the money might be spent to the greatest benefit of the islanders. As used at the Civil Service Selection Board, the object of the practice committee session is of course to help assess the relative ability of the candidates as displayed while acting as Chairman and members of a committee, but the same background story dossier and problems could be used equally well for training purposes. A topic of this kind has the advantage that the members start on precisely equal terms, since the subject matter is entirely new

to all of them—a point which is of great importance when the session is used for selection purposes but less important if it is used for training. It has the disadvantage of requiring a very considerable amount of work in preparing the file. In order to construct a satisfactory dossier, the training officer must possess a lively imagination which can think up an interesting story and also devote great attention to detail so that the facts are plausible and mutually consistent.

(3) The third method is to ask the trainees themselves to suggest a series of practical problems for discussion. Each subject would relate to an imaginary organization but would present a specific problem of a kind that is likely to be met in real life, for example:

(a) Implementing the decision to move the Head Office of a firm from London into the country, or

(b) The proposed introduction of automation into parts of a factory, which would be likely to make certain staff redundant.

When discussing a problem of this kind, the selected Chairmen would allocate roles among the other trainees, for example, General Manager (Chairman of the Committee), Personnel Manager, Office Manager, Chief Accountant, Chief Engineer, Sales Manager, and Research and Development Manager. To run the training session in this way has the considerable advantage that the trainees are able to choose their own problems and are likely to be that much more interested in discussing them. One disadvantage which is common to the second method and to this one is that, since the trainees are all required to assume parts, there must inevitably be a certain amount of play-acting which is liable to be overdone. The training officer must be able to control the effects of such over-playing. In this method particularly, one trainee may be tempted to 'invent' facts to suit his purpose, and the other trainees will not know whether they are justified in challenging them. To avoid this difficulty, it may be necessary to insist that, before discussion of any problem starts, the main 'facts' bearing on the problem are set down and agreed by all.

Each of the three methods of organizing practice committee meetings has therefore its advantages and disadvantages, and in fact the choice of topic is not of primary importance. Given a skilled training officer and a positive attitude from the trainees, any sensible topic for discussion enables the inter-play of human relationships to be practised and studied.

An example of the sort of material required for the second training method is provided by the dossier of papers relating to an imaginary Ashstone by-pass upon which are based the specimen committee meetings recorded in the Appendix. This dossier was compiled by the author for use when training in committee work, first Higher Executive Officers in a government department, and later students at L.C.C. evening classes. With each class the training sessions, each lasting $1\frac{1}{2}$ to 2 hours, were spread over several weeks, the timetable being as follows:

First week   Dossier of background information about project handed out. Trainees asked to prepare brief for Chairman.

Second week Trainees hand in their briefs for Chairman. Any questions about the background information are answered. General discussion on how to run a committee meeting.
A Chairman is chosen, and the other trainees are allocated parts.

Third week   Practice committee meeting, followed by a brief discussion of how it went. Trainees are asked to prepare minutes of the meeting.

Fourth week Trainees hand in their minutes. Full discussion of how the meeting went.

Fifth week   Discussion of the minutes and final comments on the meeting.

As training officer for these courses, during the practice committee meeting I noted the times at which each trainee spoke and the gist of his remarks, for easy reference in the subsequent discussion. This seemed sufficient, though there would be some advantage in recording the whole meeting on a tape recorder, so that one could play back any part of it as desired. This material provided many lively committee sessions. One limitation, however, was that much depended on the personality of the person chosen to act as Chairman. On the occasions when the Chairman maintained a firm grip on the meeting, presented the items for consideration clearly and kept the discussions to the point, the meetings were interesting and instructive. If the Chairman handled the meeting badly, however, little progress was made towards reaching agreement, and comments after the meeting tended to be mainly critical. On the whole, therefore, instead of having one long practice meeting as in these courses, it might be preferable to have a series of shorter meetings on the lines described in the third method, with each trainee taking his turn to act as Chairman.

THE LEYTON METHOD

The most systematic instruction specifically in handling people at committee meetings is given by Mr A. C. Leyton, Head of the Department of Social and Industrial Studies at the Northampton College of Advanced Technology, London, who has kindly discussed his training methods with me and has also allowed me to sit in at two of his practice sessions as an observer. For some years past Leyton has been running pioneer training courses, originally as Director of the Communication Training Centre of the British Association for Commercial and Industrial Education, and subsequently up and down the country on the premises of individual industrial organizations. Now he runs training courses also at the Northampton College. Briefly, his method is to form a group of (say) 8 people and to invite them to suggest 8 or more topics for discussion. If more topics are suggested than are needed, then the trainees can vote which of the possible topics they would prefer to discuss. These topics may be either industrial, for example, a meeting between Heads of Departments to discuss ways and means of increasing the labour force in order to deal with an expected increase in demand for the organization's product, or general, for example, a meeting to discuss capital punishment.

Leyton then calls upon each member of the group in turn to act as Chairman of a meeting to discuss one of the topics on the list. At the first two meetings of a series only a short time is allowed for initial consideration of the topic, so that the meeting is largely spontaneous. The idea of course is that it should be concerned less with the content of the subject matter (though this must seem real enough at the time) than with the handling of the committee members. Leyton himself takes part in the meeting as if he were an ordinary member, but his own contributions, questions and interruptions are designed either to present problems to the Chairman or to make him clarify problems which have been raised by others. Since his intention is to be provocative, he may well appear to the Chairman to be in turn rude, dumb obstinate and irrelevant. Each practice meeting lasts about 20-30 minutes, after which Leyton interrogates the Chairman as to why he reacted, or did not react, as he did to each particular situation, criticizes his handling of the meeting, and invites comments on this criticism. The discussion is recorded on a tape recorder and can be played back to illustrate and confirm points as necessary. Finally, Leyton gives his own demonstration of acting as Chairman for discussion of the last topic, and invites candid comments on it. The whole training session thus occupies some five hours, with a break in the middle.

SPECIMEN INCIDENTS

Some examples follow of the sort of situation which occurs in these training sessions and which provides suitable material for the training officer to comment on the wisdom or otherwise of the Chairman's handling of it. Throughout these examples, to avoid constant repetition, the Chairman will be referred to as C.

(A) *Maintaining Committee Proprieties*

(1) One member interrupts another while he is speaking. This is permissible only if the interruption is purely humorous (and too many 'humorous' interruptions become tedious) or if the interrupter wishes to help the speaker by e.g. putting him right on a question of fact, and if he then gives way and allows him to continue speaking. In such a case, C need do nothing. But if a speaker is interrupted solely out of impatience on the part of another member, C should immediately intervene and ask the interrupter to wait for his turn to speak.

(2) A member interrupts C while he is speaking. The same considerations apply as in situation (1), except that, out of deference to C's authority, if a member feels obliged to interrupt, he should do so apologetically. If C regards the interruption as uncalled for, he can be correspondingly severe in dealing with it.

Respect for the Chair is of the utmost importance, so that these first two situations, though they seem simple and obvious, are worth emphasizing. If one member of a Committee interrupts unnecessarily two or three times and is allowed to get away with it, it will not be long before others follow his example. The discussion will then become disorderly, with much waste of time for all members. The converse requirement of course is that, in order to retain the respect of the Committee, the Chairman must be manifestly impartial and give each member a fair chance to speak.

(3) One member interrupts while another continues speaking so that there are two people speaking at once. Wrong—to comment on what the interrupter said. Right—C ignores the interruption (whether it was a bad point or a good one) and asks the first speaker to continue.

(4) A member, Mr Smith, chats to his neighbour. Wrong—to bang angrily on the table and demand silence. Right—C asks the chatterer: 'Mr Smith, do you agree with what Mr Jones said?' If Mr Smith admits that he did not hear what Mr Jones said, C can continue: 'I will repeat what Mr Jones said . . . ' If C does this quietly but firmly, it is most

45

unlikely that Mr Smith will fail to pay attention to what is said during the rest of the meeting.

(5) A member, Mr Brown, shrugs his shoulders, laughs or throws his pencil or matches down on the table (in each case with a certain degree of rudeness). Wrong—to ignore this. Right—C says: 'I see you disagree, Mr Brown. If Mr Jones will excuse being interrupted for a moment, perhaps you will tell us why you disagree?'

(6) One member asks a question of Mr Robinson. While Mr Robinson is pausing to think how to reply, another member asks another question. Wrong—to allow the discussion to switch to this second question. Right—C cuts this second questioner short and invites Mr Robinson to reply to the first question.

(7) A member starts to answer a question addressed to the Chair. Wrong—to let him continue speaking. Right—C answers the question himself or asks another member (not necessarily the interrupter) to give his view first.

(8) One member criticizes another, e.g. for not having information available that he should have. Wrong—to comment on the justice of this criticism. Right—C turns the discussion to how the information (if relevant) can best be obtained.

(B) *Orderly Treatment of Business*

(1) A member extends the discussion outside the topic as defined by C. For example, the topic being the need for a new bus service, Mr White comments on the courtesy (or lack of it) on the part of bus conductors. Wrong—to allow further comment on Mr White's remarks. Right—C says: 'Yes, Mr White, but do you agree that there is need for a new bus service?'

(2) If C has failed to define the topic for discussion, the above situation is more likely to occur. C must check irrelevancies by saying exactly what the topic for discussion is.

(3) C asks a member to speak in vague terms such as 'Would you like to say something, Mr Jenkins?' Mr Jenkins can then hardly be blamed if he says whatever first comes

into his head, whether strictly relevant or not. Right—C asks a specific question on a definite point, e.g. 'How many more staff do you think you will need, Mr Jenkins?'

(4) A member introduces a red herring, for example, when discussing whether to recommend that a 40 m.p.h. speed limit should be imposed on a certain stretch of road, he says that all cars should be fitted with an automatic governor limiting their speed. Wrong—to allow discussion of this suggestion. Right—C says: 'That is interesting but not relevant to our present discussion. Do you favour a 40 m.p.h. speed limit on this particular stretch of road, Mr Smith?'

(5) A speaker becomes muddled and confused. Wrong—to allow another member to make fun of him. Right—C helps him out by restating his point more clearly.

(6) A speaker rambles on at length. Wrong—either to let him go on talking indefinitely or abruptly to request him to stop. Right—C pulls him up by saying: 'I gather that what you are arguing, Mr Blenkinsop, is so and so. Is that right?' (Mr Blenkinsop nods his agreement.) 'Let's have another opinion on this point. Do you agree with it, Mr Turnbull?'

(7) One member shows by what he says that he has misunderstood another member's point. C should seek to clear up the misunderstanding by restating what this point was.

(8) One member mis-states another member's views, in emotional tones. C should say, 'I don't think you have grasped Mr Brown's view correctly, Mr Jones. As I understand it, what he was saying was . . .'

(9) The discussion begins to ramble. Wrong—either to let it ramble on or to terminate it without any conclusion having been reached. Right—C intervenes to remind the committee of the points that needed to be settled; he sums up the position reached, the points agreed and the points still needing to be resolved.

(10) A member proposes something *ultra vires*. Wrong—C lets the motion be discussed. Right—C points this out and obtains a rewording of the proposition.

(11) A member makes a vague suggestion, e.g. that 'There ought to be a scheme of compensation for workers in the factory losing their jobs through automation. Wrong—to

allow further general comments on this vague proposal. Right—C asks: 'What sort of a scheme had you in mind, Mr Jones? How much compensation are you suggesting?'

(12) If C allows a member to switch the discussion to another, quite different topic, this will irritate the other members. One likely reaction is that an aggressive member, who feels cross but does not wish to be rude to the Chairman, will take it out on another weaker member by telling him to shut up.

(13) A member proposes a resolution which is not clearly worded. Wrong—C puts it to the vote: later another member raises a point which shows he is not clear what the resolution said or implied. Right—C rephrases the resolution to make it clear and secures the consent of the proposer that this resolution be put to the vote.

(14) C fails to make clear what has been agreed on one item before proceeding to the next item on the agenda. Later in the meeting someone will probably ask what was agreed, or deliberately revert to the previous item, in which case the discussion will start all over again.

(15) C lets the meeting tail off inconclusively. Instead of doing this, he should summarise the action to be taken and by whom.

(C) *Forming the Best Group View*

(1) C presents his own views strongly at the beginning of a discussion. If he does this, it will either inhibit the discussion or provoke strong opposition from certain members which the Chairman, having abandoned his position of impartiality, will find it difficult or impossible to control. In either case a genuine agreed group view is unlikely to emerge.

(2) C terminates many items by saying that he will look into the matter and see what can be done. Preferably facts should have been investigated before the meeting. If further research is needed, tasks should be shared among members of the committee.

(3) One person hogs the meeting. Sometimes, the best course

for C, when a later item is reached, may be to ask for views in turn round the table, starting just beyond the offender, so that his turn to speak comes last.

(4) There is prolonged opposition to the general view from a particular member. Wrong—C allows other members to harden his opposition by blunt criticism. Right—C secures his acquiescence by praising and adopting part of what he said, then pointing out why the rest was not practicable.

(5) A person posing as an 'expert' states something as a fact which is not really proven. Wrong—to let this statement pass at the time but to query it later. Right—C immediately questions the 'expert's' assumptions and, by encouraging other members to state their views on the topic, enables the point to remain open.

(6) After lengthy discussion of an item, a member loses patience and calls for a vote on the item, even though not all the relevant points have been mentioned. Wrong—C agrees and puts the matter to the vote. Supporters of the minority view will be angry and continue to argue the matter. Right—C says that the discussion has gone on for some time and many points have been discussed: if members have any fresh points to raise, could they please do so briefly. Then, if a vote has to be taken, C can be firm in saying that this item has been dealt with and he will not allow discussion of it to be reopened.

(7) C sums up discussion of a proposition in accordance with the number of speakers on each side, giving no particular weight to a powerful minority view from an influential member. It would be better for C to invite other members' comments on this view before summing up.

(8) After presentation of strongly opposing views, C proposes an obvious and feeble compromise. For example, if the subject of controversy at a Parochial Church Council meeting is which of two senior members should have the honour of moving a vote of thanks to a visiting Bishop, a feeble compromise would be to suggest that each speaks in turn. It might be preferable for C to resolve the deadlock by suggesting that on this occasion the honour be bestowed on

another, comparatively junior, member of the Church Council.

SOME GENERAL COMMENTS ON TRAINING

It will be seen that the foregoing examples of incidents that occur at practice committee sessions and are worth commenting on have been grouped under three headings:

(A) Maintaining Committee Proprieties.

(B) Orderly Treatment of Business.

(C) Forming the Best Group View.

Incidents of type A are the most obvious and, if a series of practice meetings are held by the same group of trainees, the training officer may find it best to concentrate on them during the first one or two meetings, so that subsequent meetings are at least run with due regard to committee proprieties. Some of the personal antagonisms, interruptions, etc., at these practice sessions are more outspoken than is usual at most committee meetings (though they do occur sometimes in real life). Any trainee notices the overt signs of discord and learns how to deal with them. This helps him later to recognize signs of potential discord when covert and to take appropriate action in time to prevent the potential discord from developing and wrecking the committee.

When discussing the next few sessions, the training officer can then concentrate on incidents of type B and endeavour to build up a technique of promoting orderly progression of thought. Incidents of type (C) are the most complex, calling for skill and subtlety on the part of the Chairman, in addition to mastery of technique. It may be easy, for example, for the Chairman to realize that after presentation of strongly opposing views, as in incident (C8), some 'integrated' solution is required and not a mere compromise. It may be much harder for him to decide how such an 'integrated' solution can best be arrived at.

At the initial practice sessions, particularly with trainees inexperienced in committee work, the training officer may have to intervene frequently with comments designed to stir the meeting up, or with questions such as 'Excuse me, Mr Chairman, but I am still not quite clear what we have agreed. Could you please enlighten me?' intended to make the Chairman ask himself if he is doing his job properly. At later practice sessions, when the trainees will have profited from each other's experience, the Chairman will become increasingly competent, and the training officer should have less need to intervene. He can however become increasingly candid in his comments during the post-mortems on the practice sessions.

There is one valuable point which Leyton stresses during the training sessions which he runs. Some Chairmen tend to make themselves the focus of discussion throughout a meeting. That is to say, the Chairman asks member A for his views and then comments on them, asks member B a question and thanks him for his reply, puts a further point to member D and so on, so that the order of speaking is C-A-C-B-C-D-C-E, etc. This inevitably makes for a dull meeting, with not more than two members participating in it at any one moment. It is far better for the Chairman to strive to keep the discussion flowing in a variety of directions. Instead of himself commenting on member A's suggestion, he could ask member B to say whether he agrees, and this might induce member K to volunteer his comments. The order of speaking might thus be C-A-B-K-X-F-C, etc. The discussion is lively, with all members actively participating and several seeking to catch the Chairman's eye.

VALUE OF PRACTICE SESSIONS

There can be no doubt in the minds of people who attend these practice committee sessions or a variety of real life committees that different Chairmen differ enormously in their skill in handling meetings. It is less evident perhaps whether these individual differences are mainly innate—some people being naturally much better at chairing committees than others are—or largely susceptible to training and experience. Some research into this point would be both interesting and useful in interpreting the evidence of the practice sessions, but, whatever the outcome of the research, the sessions must have value either for selection or for training purposes. If the differences are mainly innate, then it is important to classify the people according to their skill in handling meetings and whenever possible to give preference to the more skilled persons when selecting committee Chairmen. If this skill can be acquired, then it is important that all Chairmen should be helped to acquire it by being given appropriate training. On either hypothesis, the practice sessions could be of great value, and it is to be hoped that Leyton's methods will be developed and spread all over the country.

6

ROLE OF THE CHAIRMAN

The Chairman's role will depend upon the type of Committee and especially upon the method of discussion used by the committee, c.f. chapter 4. If a meeting is of the free, leaderless type, the Chairman will have little authority except to preside and keep order. Conversely, if a meeting has precise agenda and objectives, the Chairman will have to play a dominant part in order to get the business settled according to schedule. This chapter will be concerned, in the main, with meetings where the method of discussion is of an intermediate kind. It is assumed that the meeting is not necessarily tied to a rigid agenda or timetable, and that the Chairman has authority, for example, to decide who shall speak next. The Chairman's role is thus important and permits some flexibility, within his own discretion.

Opinions differ as to the part that the Chairman should play at meetings of this kind. According to one school of thought he can make his most effective contribution if he acts as group 'leader'. One argument is that by virtue of his position he is likely to be particularly well placed as regards obtaining information relevant to items to be discussed and so, provided he does his 'homework' before the meeting, he should know more about the subject matter than most, perhaps all, other members of the committee. It is therefore reasonable and desirable that the Chairman should form a provisional view on each item before the meeting. Unless the pros and cons are so delicately balanced that he feels quite undecided, he should be prepared to give a lead in what he considers the right direction, though he should not press his view unduly if the majority of the committee argue against it.

In practice, one disadvantage of this conception of the Chairman's role is that in the effort to give a definite lead the Chairman is liable to talk too much himself. He may forget that the purpose of setting up a committee is to draw upon the collective experience and wisdom of members and use the meeting as a sounding board for his own opinions. For example, the Chairman of a recent high-powered committee was a practised and accomplished speaker, who from the outset did most of the talking. This prompted another member of the committee to keep notes over a period. He found that the Chairman was speaking eighty per cent of the time when the committee were having private discussions, and sixty per cent of the time when they were supposed to be hearing the views of outsiders. Three members of the committee were so irritated that they threatened to resign in protest against the Chairman's method of running the committee. It is a tribute to the co-operativeness of these members that they were persuaded to stay on, and eventually the committee produced a unanimous report.

Another Chairman, who was the head of an organization, had a special technique which must have disconcerted new members of his committees. His custom, when taking each new item of importance on the agenda, was to gaze at a committee member, summarize what he understood to be that individual's views on the topic and then ask if he had made a fair statement. After repeating this process with each member in turn, he would give his own views on the topic and finally sum up on behalf of the meeting. This particular Chairman's knowledge both of the subject matter for discussion and of the individuals was so great that the other members were seldom able to criticize his statement of what he believed to be their views, or to suggest improvements on his summing up. Nevertheless, this technique is not recommended for general adoption.

The foregoing examples are perhaps somewhat extreme, but many Chairmen who are no more conceited or egotistical than are most of us, and whose earnest desire is to be of the greatest service, fail to run their committees smoothly and efficiently because of their mistaken concept of leadership. They visualize leading a committee in terms of presenting the pros and cons of a matter, recommending the best course of action and securing group approval of it by a combination of their own persuasive argument and personal dominance. Ideally in their view, the trust and confidence which the other members of the group come to place in the leader are such that they are half-way towards accepting any proposal which he recommends to them. In a peace-time context at any rate, this concept of the paternal leader does not work out in practice. If the Chairman consistently dominates all meetings, this fact will in time be resented by the other members, who will feel, rightly, that they are not pulling their weight. Some general principles of leadership have been admirably described by Mary Parker Follett.[1] In her view, the leader should make people feel their responsibility, not take it from them, and should encourage them to participate to the best of their ability. The best leader asks people to serve, not him, but the common end. Leadership does not require a dominant, aggressive personality, but knowledge of the job, sincerity, and imagination to see ahead. The leader gets an order followed, first because men really do want to do things in the right way and he can show them that way, and secondly because he too is obeying —his own example is of great importance. Applying these general principles to the committee situation, it follows that the Chairman should not attempt to tell a committee what they should do or how they should think. His role is not to lay down the law, to criticize or to pass judgment, but to encourage the committee to think for itself, to voice its thought freely, and through the interchange of ideas to move towards the solution of its problems. He leads, not by dominating, but by helping the committee to make use of its own experience, and by guiding the discussion so that group conclusions are reached.

According to another school of thought, the Chairman should act mainly or entirely as 'moderator' of the committee. If he has any strong views of his own, he should certainly suppress them. His function is not to give a lead, but to hold the ring, to allow all points of view to be expressed freely and to enable a group view to emerge. He should act

[1] *Dynamic Administration* (Bath Management Publications Trust Ltd.), 1941.

as mouthpiece for the meeting and not reveal his own opinions. The following example illustrates the remarkable extent to which a Chairman can be self-effacing if he considers this to be his duty. At the initial meetings of an industrial Trade Association widely different views were expressed, and there seemed to be some danger of a split on the committee. The Chairman expressed no opinions of his own but kept the discussion amicable and to the point until eventually agreement was reached. A report had to be made to the Governing Body of the Trade Association. The Chairman summed up what appeared to be the committee view, then surprised the committee by stating that he personally disagreed with it. He suggested that someone else ought to present the report, but the other members unanimously said that they would like him to do so.

For the Chairman to be completely self-effacing, however, or, as in the previous example, to reveal his own views only after the group decision had been reached, seems a waste when he has special knowledge or experience to place at the disposal of the committee. Moreover, by taking an active part and throwing in his own weight when the arguments voiced within the group seem to him overwhelmingly in one direction, the Chairman can assist the reaching of agreement. In short, in most committee situations, neither school of thought is entirely right. It is not satisfactory for the Chairman either to be dominant all the time or to keep in the background all the time. On the contrary, he must be flexible in his handling. In general, he can afford to guide with a light rein early in the proceedings, allowing other members to have their say. When discussion has gone on long enough, however, the Chairman must be able to take a strong line and make a clear summing-up. In other words he must be two-faced.

GUIDING THE GROUP DISCUSSION

The smooth working of the committee depends on the Chairman's knowledge and skill in—

(1) Explaining clearly what the topics for discussion are, making each topic as specific as possible. Particularly if the

A Two-Faced Chairman

time for discussion is limited, it is vital that the Chairman should define the topic precisely, so as to focus attention on the relevant issues. The Chairman at a Residents Association committee meeting, for example, might introduce the next item for discussion by saying: 'The topic for consideration is whether we can support the request from residents in the new Parkside housing estate to have a bus service provided along Parkside Avenue. It is not for us to say now whether the need could be met by diversion of an existing service or whether a new service would be required—still less, to comment on the adequacy or otherwise of existing services in the neighbourhood, interesting though this topic may be—but simply to assess the extent of the need, that is to say how many people would be likely to take advantage of a bus service along Parkside Avenue if one were provided.'

(2) Seeing that each interested party has the opportunity to speak, without anybody being too long-winded.

(3) Seeing that only one person speaks at once, and stopping unnecessary interruptions.

(4) Keeping people more or less to the point, but never giving the impression of being in a hurry. A member has *not* the right to have discussion of any point he raises, but he is likely to feel resentful if the Chairman states bluntly that the point is irrelevant or not worth discussing. It is preferable for the Chairman to dispose of the point with tact and a little humour. One experienced Chairman, for example, when some red herring was introduced, would use a phrase such as: 'That is an interesting point, but perhaps rather a refinement', and thus redirect the discussion without giving offence.

(5) Giving full and courteous attention to each contribution, striving constantly to understand it rather than to evaluate it in terms of his own opinions.

(6) Helping to interpret each member's contribution, sometimes by restatement, so that nobody misunderstands anybody else. It is better, if necessary, to reopen a point rather than to pass on to another topic if it appears that the point may not have been generally understood. This technique incidentally can be helpful for deflating somebody who is inclined to be a pompous windbag. I remember one occasion when the meeting was considering how to handle someone outside the committee who had been raising unnecessary difficulties. One committee member spoke at length to the effect that it would be necessary to deal firmly with this person and to show him that the committee would not tolerate any nonsense, yet at the same time by speaking tactfully and persuasively to avoid being rude or giving offence, etc., etc. At this point, the Chairman summed up his advice by saying 'In other words, Mr Smith, you would advise using the mailed fist in a velvet glove', and indeed this was all that his lengthy contribution amounted to. Mr Smith could only nod his head and spoke no more on this item.

(7) Judging a contribution, when evaluation is called for, by its content and not by the persuasiveness with which it was delivered.

(8) Relieving the tension when two members are in danger of falling out by intervening, e.g. to point out some way in which they are agreed, or by shifting the subject slightly with a touch of humour.

(9) Deciding when discussion of an item has gone on long enough. The Chairman can then either call on a member who has been prominent in the discussion to suggest a resolution to be put to the meeting or do this himself. It is often a help if the Chairman has prepared in advance a timetable of roughly how many minutes can be spent on each item—not with a view to enforcing strict adherence to this all the time, but so that from time to time he can check whether the meeting is running more or less to schedule. If the meeting is fixed to end at a certain time, e.g. at 1.15 p.m. for lunch, this precaution helps to avoid an unseemly and unproductively wild rush in the closing minutes, with the later propositions not properly resolved. As regards items, the outcome of which can be foreseen with tolerable confidence, the Chairman can save time and help to keep the meeting running smoothly by having some likely resolutions prepared in advance. If the discussion takes an unexpected course, however, he may have to modify his draft resolution or replace it with another prepared on the spur of the moment.

(10) Seeing that any resolution put to the meeting is both clear and worded in such a way as to stand the best chance of securing general agreement. This is definitely the Chairman's responsibility, and, until he is satisfied in both these respects, he should not put a resolution to the meeting, even if he is being pressed hard to do so, but should explain why the wording of the resolution is imperfect and suggest how it might be improved. A member who wishes to have put to the meeting what is obviously a minority view should if possible be dissuaded from pressing the issue to a vote. In the last resort, however, he is entitled to insist upon a vote if he can find a seconder for his proposal, or upon having his minority view noted in the minutes of the meeting.

(11) Before the committee moves on from one item to the

next, stating what has and what has not been agreed, so that nobody is in any doubt about this.

(12) Considering the practical application of the group view.

(13) Indicating what action, if any, is to be taken, e.g. that the secretary will send a letter to so and so.

EXTENT TO WHICH HE CAN VOICE HIS OWN VIEWS

The question then arises as to what extent, if any, the Chairman should voice his own views. If he can succeed in steering the discussion so that complete agreement is reached without his having to do so, so much the better. He can then sum up the discussion and state the group decision with which he personally concurs. If all the relevant points have been brought out in the discussion, there is no need for him to add anything else. If however an additional argument occurs to him, there is some advantage in his mentioning this in consolidation of the group decision. If there is disagreement among committee members on some controversial issue, it may sometimes be helpful for the Chairman to intervene by giving his own views. He should never do so early in the discussion, nor should he ever state them in an extreme or dogmatic form which a shy committee member might find it embarrassing to contradict. Above all, he should make it crystal clear, if he does intervene in this way, that he is for the moment voicing his personal opinion and not purporting to sum up the group view.

Another occasion on which the Chairman may decide to play a positive part is when after prolonged discussion the group seems in agreement except for a single member who seems inclined to hold out against the rest. The Chairman may then suggest to this member that, if he is satisfied that his own point of view has been considered thoroughly and yet all other members of the group take a contrary view, he might feel able to acquiesce in what the others think. If he decides to use the authority of his office to act in this way, however, the Chairman must remember that it doesn't pay to bludgeon people or to force a member to agree to something against his will, leaving him overborne rather than convinced. In this event the member is likely either to re-open the matter at a subsequent meeting, or to fail to persuade his superiors that he was right to agree, in which case he will be overruled by them. Constant patience and perseverance are therefore essential. If deadlock is reached and an immediate decision is not required, it may help to suggest 'let's draft a memorandum clarifying the points at issue', or to take some other action to reduce the temperature. Some people are reluctant to agree to things orally and like to see them set down in black and white. To submit a memorandum helps such people.

HANDLING AWKWARD COMMITTEE MEMBERS

(a) Unpunctual Members

As a matter of courtesy, all members of a committee should endeavour to arrive on time for a meeting if they possibly can, neither late nor more than a very few minutes early. If some of them fail to do so, the Chairman will have to consider how to deal with the situation. If at the appointed time one or more members have failed to arrive, the Chairman will have to decide whether it is better to delay the start, thus wasting the time of all who did arrive punctually, or to start promptly with the penalty that latecomers will not know what has been said unless the Chairman summarizes the early points specially for their benefit. The Chairman's action will probably depend upon the relative importance of the contribution likely to be made by a latecomer to the early items. Sometimes he may decide after a few minutes' wait that the meeting must start, but that a particular item had better be deferred until a particular member has arrived. When a latecomer does arrive he will probably be expecting some reproof, and the Chairman can deal more effectively with the situation in some other way.

An amusing technique was that employed by Spencer Furnivall, the Prime Minister in Harold Nicholson's *Public Faces* (page 66). When a minister arrived late for a Cabinet meeting he would at first affect not to notice his arrival, and then turn round and say: 'Are we all here now? Bullinger? Ah, yes, there you are! Now we had better begin'—without giving the late arrival a chance to deliver his carefully rehearsed excuse for being late.

Almost as tiresome as the people who habitually arrive late for a committee meeting are the people who habitually arrive unduly early, since this makes it more difficult for the Chairman and Secretary to complete their preparations for the meeting.

(b) Over-talkative Members

Sometimes a new committee member talks too much through sheer inexperience, just as others are silent for the same reason. At the first committee meeting that he attends a person may try hard to be helpful by saying something on each item—he may feel that this is expected of him. Most people quickly become aware when their comments are or are not appreciated, and learn to ration their remarks, to speak only when they have something material to contribute to the discussion which is unlikely to be said better by anybody else. Some people, however, persist in talking too much.

If an over-talkative member habitually talks poor sense, the other members will spontaneously combine to discipline him. The difficult problem arises if he talks good sense but is consistently quick off the mark, so that other members get little chance to speak. If the Chairman knows that one member, Mr Smith, is particularly talkative and foresees trouble through his talking too much at a meeting, he may be able to avoid this by placing late on the agenda (say as item 8) the topic of particular interest to Mr Smith. Then if Mr Smith starts to talk too much on earlier items, the Chairman can say: 'This is all very interesting, but I am anxious to leave plenty of time for item 8, which I believe is of particular interest to you, Mr Smith, so you may not want to spend too long discussing this item'. In general, if at a meeting one member is talking too much, it may help for the Chairman to break the discussion up into separate items (or principles and detailed points), inviting different people to speak first for different items. Otherwise how soon the Chairman can tactfully break in and ask another member for his views must depend upon how long the talkative person can speak without pausing for breath.

(c) *Silent Members*

In contrast, there is the member who does not speak at all. This may be for one of a variety of reasons, for example, inexperience, shyness, slowness in discussion, or lack of desire to participate. If a member is silent through lack of experience, the Chairman will be well advised to leave him alone for the time being. Later when the Chairman thinks that the inexperienced member has found his feet, he can tactfully suggest that the committee would welcome a fresh viewpoint from a new or comparatively new member and invite his opinion on some not too obscure or controversial matter.

Among established committee members, however, it is desirable that all should contribute from time to time. This is not to say that all should necessarily speak to an equal extent. It is logical and desirable that members with more knowledge and experience should speak more than members with lesser qualifications. But it is not desirable that any member should over a prolonged period make no spoken contribution whatever, and it is one of the Chairman's duties to notice if this happens and to consider what, if anything, he should do about it. If the silent member is merely shy or lacking in self-confidence, the Chairman can endeavour to draw him out. The other members will usually co-operate. He might, for example, be asked, prior to a meeting, if he would second a motion for re-election. If he did this successfully, it would help him to come out of his shell on future occasions.

Very often, however, a member is habitually silent, not because he is shy or because he has nothing to say, but because he takes time to collect his thoughts and is slow to get off the mark in discussion. During a committee meeting, therefore, he may keep on intending to speak, but each time somebody else forestalls him and makes much the same point that he was intending to make. He may have the good sense to realize that the point has been made and is not worth repeating, and yet feel frustrated that he is apparently making no contribution to the discussion other than nodding his head from time to time or perhaps saying, 'Yes, I agree' or 'No, I don't see that'. It is particularly important that the Chairman should notice when this is happening and do something about it. He may be aware, for instance, that Mr Jones, though not a fluent speaker, is a pleasant person, liked and respected by all, who chats quite freely when with two or three companions, but has not a quick mind and is unlikely, at a committee meeting, ever to be the first person to think of a fresh point. His judgment may be sound, however, and his opinions well worth having when the pros and cons of a matter have been presented. The Chairman might be well advised, therefore, to keep it in mind to call upon Mr Jones to give his views towards the end of the discussion of an item, particularly if opinions on the point seem fairly evenly divided and a fresh, carefully considered, view would be helpful.

Here is an example of the potentially useful contribution of a 'silent' member: a certain high-level committee was considering a new scheme for radical reorganization in the field of education. After lengthy discussion and debate as to the theoretical advantages and disadvantages of the new scheme the meeting had not reached agreement. The Chairman noticed that one of the members, Mr Green, had said nothing. Knowing him to be a practical man with relevant experience and likely to have a good idea of how ordinary people would react to the proposal, the Chairman asked Mr Green whether he favoured the new scheme. Mr Green replied: 'Well, theoretically it sounds all right, but I have spent a fortnight discussing the scheme with my wife and I can't persuade her that it would work'. Further discussion followed, but Mr Green's objection was probably decisive in causing the committee to reject the proposal.

Finally a member may remain silent, not through shyness, inexperience or lack of verbal facility, but for the opposite reasons. He may be an experienced person who has served on committees for many years and has joined in discussions similar to most of those which take place on the present committee. On many topics, the circumstances may have altered so that new conclusions are required, but such a person may have difficulty in appreciating this. He is liable to feel that these matters are really not worth discussing all over again; that if they must be raised at all the committee ought to turn to him for a few crisp words presenting the main issues and the only sensible conclusion to which the committee should come; but, if the committee have not the wit to turn to him for advice, he doesn't see why he should bother to intervene. In short, he has become stale and largely incapable of participation in the work of the committee. In a few cases, if this member has particularly valuable experience, it may be worth the Chairman's while to go out of his way to seek his opinion directly an item comes up for discussion, saying that in view of his experience the committee would find his advice particularly useful. More often, however, retirement from the committee is the best solution.

METHODS OF FACILITATING AGREEMENT

A Chairman can often do a great deal to keep everybody happy by 'mingling' before a meeting opens, particularly with those who do not contribute much except by their presence. They sometimes blossom if they are taken notice of. Here the Secretary also can be a great help.

In order to assist the committee to reach sensible decisions, good *timing* by the Chairman is essential: sweet reason by itself is not enough. For example, the Executive of a certain professional association had for months been conducting negotiations with the employers about pay and conditions and had become persuaded that the employer's final offer, though not all that had been hoped for, was the best that could be obtained in the circumstances. At an open meeting of the association various speakers opposed the Executive view on emotional grounds and tempers became frayed. At this point the Chairman wisely adjourned the meeting for a tea break. This allowed time for informal discussions and reflection while tempers cooled. After the adjournment the chief spokesman for the Executive explained the difficulties and obtained a sympathetic hearing and endorsement of the Executive proposals.

On another occasion at the meeting of a small working party, member A made one proposal. Member B criticized it and put forward a counter-proposal. Two hours were spent in which A criticized the second proposal and B criticized the first, while the other two members were confused and embarrassed. No progress was made. Indeed, so long as the discussion concentrated on the faults of these two schemes, no progress was possible. After a break for lunch, A and B settled the whole thing amicably in five minutes. They agreed that both schemes were faulty, and together worked out a new and simpler scheme.

When two members of a committee, or two groups of members, seem at loggerheads, part of the trouble may be caused by the fact that each party is so preoccupied with (what seem to it to be) the virtues of its own proposals that it fails to pay any attention to the counter-proposals of the opposing party but keeps on referring back to its own. This state of affairs has been apparent, for instance, at some of the international disarmament conferences between Western and Eastern representatives. Each side has come to the conference with proposals which seemed to it eminently reasonable and to afford an appropriate basis for agreement if the other side really wished to reach agreement. Unfortunately the two sets of proposals were so different that no real contact was achieved between them, and each side accused the other of not genuinely seeking agreement because it did not consider its own proposals seriously. It has been suggested that, to avoid this lack of contact (which can be observed also at some 'joint' committee meetings), it would be desirable for the two sides to agree beforehand that at the first meeting A's proposals will be presented and discussion will be centred entirely on them. The other side will be encouraged to ask questions designed to clarify the proposals and, when they are entirely clear, to comment on them, but not to refer to their own counter-proposals as such. At the second meeting B's proposals will be presented and discussion similarly will be concerned solely with them. This technique might indeed help to ensure that each side at least considered the other's proposals seriously, and the process could be continued until some measure of understanding had been reached. The technique is hardly likely to be practicable, however, unless there is a strong Chairman, at once manifestly impartial and determined to see that each set of proposals receives fair treatment and that the side criticizing them sticks to the rules of the arrangement and does not, for example, criticize points which have not been made by the other side. Given a strong impartial Chairman, however, and willingness on the part of both sides to abide by his rulings, it is arguable that a formal arrangement to consider each set of proposals at alternate meetings would not be necessary. It might be sufficient for the Chairman to state at each meeting exactly which proposal was to be considered next and to see that all speakers stuck to this particular item until it had been discussed thoroughly.

A further extension of the process of giving serious consideration to your opponent's point of view is called 'role-reversal technique'.[1] This technique means that the Chairman calls on each protagonist to do his best to state the arguments of his opponent and to refrain from pressing his own case until he has done so. In certain circumstances, e.g. in matrimonial disputes where there is much fundamental goodwill and genuine misunderstanding, this process serves to reduce belligerence and promote better understanding as the prerequisite to agreement. In a committee situation this technique would be difficult to apply without the ready co-operation of the other committee members, which implies some degree of sophistication on their part. Here again, however, an experienced and skilful Chairman might employ the essence of role-reversal without formally proclaiming that he was about to use this technique. He could, for example, call on the member making a statement and the member opposing it to turn from the statement itself (or its denial) to the assumptions underlying the statement, and to discuss the correctness or reasonableness of these assumptions.

[1] See 'The Technique of Role-Reversal' by Professor J. Cohen, in *Occupational Psychology*, 1951.

Sometimes it might turn out that an assumption which one member regarded as 'common knowledge' would be challenged by his opponent. In this case the Chairman could ask the other members of the committee for their views on this assumption and concentrate discussion on it until a substantial measure of agreement had been reached among all members, including the original protagonists. Applying this step-by-step process of submitting all the alleged 'facts' and the various assumptions on both sides to critical scrutiny, the Chairman and the rest of the committee might eventually succeed in persuading one or both of the protagonists to alter their attitudes sufficiently to make agreement between them possible.

7

ADVICE TO A NEW MEMBER

A person inexperienced in committees may well ask himself the question: 'How can I make the most useful contribution to a committee which I have been asked to join?' If so, the following advice may be useful to him:

PLAN DEGREES OF INVOLVEMENT

Decide how involved you wish to become in the work of the committee and how much time you can spare.

(a) If you are not really interested, decline the invitation. Be firm. If necessary, say that you expect to be going abroad shortly!

(b) If you are moderately interested, join the committee and attend regularly but decline invitations to take on any heavier burden. One thing leads to another, and, if you innocently agree to become Assistant Treasurer (nothing to do except when the Treasurer is away!) or Social Secretary (only one dinner a year, old boy!) this year, you may find that in five years time you will have become General Secretary and overburdened with work.

(c) If you are really interested (and would not mind becoming in due course Chairman or General Secretary), attend all meetings, volunteer for sub-committees and accept any reasonable tasks on behalf of the committee.

Study the constitution of the committee and the rules of procedure that apply to it. Learn the powers of the committee and the ways in which it can make its views known. Much time can be wasted in:

(a) Discussions that are repetitive or out of order—all members should be aware, for instance, that if a member moves an amendment to a motion and succeeds in getting it seconded, this amendment must be voted on before the substantive motion can be put to the vote.

(b) Proposing action which is either *ultra vires* or unlikely to lead to any fruitful result, e.g. writing to the local M.P. on trivial issues or to the wrong level of an organisation.

DISCRETION IN SPEAKING

Be regular in attendance. It is very helpful when an item comes up to be able to recall what was said about it on a previous occasion; and it is correspondingly irritating to your colleagues if you start to air your views in obvious ignorance that precisely the same points were made and dealt with on some previous occasion. At the very least, attend alternate meetings so that if you miss a meeting you hear the minutes read or discussed at the next meeting, become aware of what has been decided, and have a chance to query any point before it becomes stale. If you cannot attend at least half the meetings, it is better to resign from the committee.

Be punctual and, unless circumstances make this absolutely impossible, stay until the end of a meeting. This shows respect for the committee and enables you to get to know the members better in informal conversation before and after the meeting. I recall one fairly senior civil servant who was notorious for his habit of arriving late at a meeting and also leaving early, muttering in each case apologies for being excessively busy. It was suspected that he did this in order to emphasize his own importance, and he was cordially disliked in consequence.

Keep awake, especially while minutes or letters are being read, and try to catch at least the name of the person who wrote the letter. I remember one disastrous occasion when a letter was read out aloud at a committee meeting. It seemed to me to contain both errors of fact and faulty inferences and I said as much. Judge my embarrassment when someone at the meeting (who was an old friend of mine) got up and complained that my remarks seemed candid to the point of rudeness, and I discovered that he was in fact the author of the letter.

If you are a new member of a Standing Committee, be careful not to say very much until you have attended a

Don't Fall Asleep

number of meetings and feel well established. The best opportunity for making a useful contribution may come when an item crops up of which you have special knowledge or experience, e.g. the upkeep of roads if you happen to be a building contractor or an educational problem if you happen to be both a schoolteacher and a parent. In addition to knowing something about the subject matter, it is desirable, before you speak and make positive suggestions, to have become aware of the 'feel' of the committee, i.e. the sort of way in which it likes to conduct its business.

PARTICIPATION IN A WORKING GROUP

The following comments are particularly applicable to a working group of homogeneous composition and flexible methods so that each member has a chance to speak but is not entitled by virtue of his position to override the views of others.

Note that a working group needs several 'self-starters', i.e. people with a fund of ideas (good or bad). To have good ideas is not enough, however. In order to influence the committee, you must learn to present your ideas to your colleagues in such a way that they have a fair chance of being accepted as the group view.

Bear in mind that your influence on the group is likely to depend upon four factors:

(a) Your background knowledge. The 'authority' of anything you say will depend on this.

(b) Your own ability and fund of ideas, original and constructive rather than critical.

(c) Your own personality—not so much your dominance (though up to a point this helps) as the extent to which you inspire confidence. As important as having a good idea is patience and determination to persevere with a proposal until some part of it is implemented. To quote from a well-known letter to Queen Elizabeth from Sir Francis Drake: 'There must be a beginning of any good matter, but the continuing to the end, until it be thoroughly finished, yields the true glory'.

(d) Your co-operativeness and willingness to work in with other people, while remaining true to your own principles.

TACT AND COURTESY TOWARDS COLLEAGUES

Even when well established in the committee, do not try to dominate a meeting by talking too much. Avoid frequent repetitions of 'I think', 'My view is'. As far as possible quote remarks by other members, facts from reports, etc., in support of what you are saying. If you wish to say a lot about one item which to you seems important, say little about the other, less important items. It is sometimes possible to settle minor points before or after the meeting, so that at the meeting the points you raise are all major ones.

Look for the good in other members' contributions. If you must disagree with one point, preface your disagreement by agreeing on some other point. Always give credit for what the other member was trying to say, and do not criticize his way of saying it, or say anything which would make him seem small.

Avoid taking sides in an argument or doing anything to widen a split within the committee. You can agree with one person without ridiculing the ideas of another.

While you are entitled to query facts that seem to you doubtful, avoid flat contradictions of opinion. It is better to say something like: 'I would put this rather differently . . . '

Study how much weight your various colleagues carry. Be particularly chary of opposing the views of someone of particular authority unless you are absolutely assured of the facts. If this is so and you are convinced your views are sound, then speak firmly and confidently. If your opponent deserves the authority he carries, he will be prepared to acknowledge the merits of a well-presented case, however opposed to his own first opinion.

Decide beforehand which features of any proposal are essential and which are inessential features on which you are prepared to give way.

8

INFLUENCING OTHER PEOPLE

SYMPATHETIC UNDERSTANDING THE FIRST ESSENTIAL

Earlier chapters have considered committee meetings from the point of view of getting the best results out of a group, with all members contributing to the best of their ability and showing as much readiness to listen to the views of others as to speak themselves. In this chapter, meetings are considered from the point of view of an individual member who wishes to influence and persuade people to take the particular decision that he favours. To such a person, the influencing of other people through personal contact is the whole *raison d'être* of a committee meeting, since his business might otherwise be settled equally well and more economically of time by exchange of correspondence or telephone calls. He must remember that people are not wholly or even mainly rational in thought or outlook. The mere orderly presentation of facts whether in a paper or at a meeting is not enough. His first endeavour, when introducing his case, should be to win his colleagues' assent that the item is worth discussing at all and sympathy with the line that he is taking. Then he must seek to secure not only their agreement that his arguments are sound but their co-operation in getting appropriate action taken in consequence. To have any chance of fulfilling these aims, he must obviously get to know his fellow committee members as people. The question then arises whether to do anything more than this is legitimate, desirable or expedient. Opinions differ, but the general view seems to be that the best 'tactics' are well worth careful consideration, bearing in mind that tactics, once they are apparent, are often self-defeating.

LOBBYING BEFORE A MEETING

The desirability or otherwise of prior consultation or

'lobbying' people before a meeting is a point of particular interest. One can contrast, for example, the somewhat legalistic advice of R. W. Bell[1]—lobby people only in order to avoid genuine misunderstandings—and the cynical but practical advice of C. Northcote Parkinson[2] — carefully planned and resolute lobbying is essential in order to capture the votes of the undecided centre bloc. One's attitude to the ethics of prior consultation is likely to depend very much on the circumstances and on the phraseology used to describe the form of consultation. Inviting another committee member out to lunch, for instance, can be described as showing 'Desire to explore in a relaxed situation the full implication of items to be discussed' or in less flattering terms. On the whole, one might say that the process of getting together beforehand to discuss the issues and reach preliminary agreement, as described in C. P. Snow's *The Masters*, is either a very good sign (if the aim is simply to save time) or a very bad sign (indicating feuds).

Subject to the above reservations on the desirability of prior consultation, some general advice is as follows:

(1) In order to get an idea of how much agreement at a meeting is likely to be practicable, it is often helpful to sound one or two members at an early stage. They will usually be flattered by being consulted. If one does consult them, however, it follows that one must normally be willing to be influenced by their advice.

(2) A fellow member may be known to be:

(*a*) Favourably disposed towards the proposal. If so, prior consultation is likely to serve two purposes:

   (*i*) As regards the main argument, the other member may be able to suggest a rearrangement of ideas or a different method of presentation that is more likely to be acceptable;

   (*ii*) He may make detailed criticisms of a constructive nature.

The originator would be well advised to note any telling

[1] *Be Sure You Agree* (Allen & Unwin, 1960).
[2] *Parkinson's Law* (John Murray, 1958).

75

phrases and incorporate them, with due acknowledgment, in his own presentation. The other member is then more likely to act as an ally.

(b) Unfavourably disposed. If so, the main object will be to clarify points of difference. Some may be points of misunderstanding, which can be cleared up. Others may be points of real difference. It will help the originator to be aware of these and consider before the meeting:

(i) The points on which he will be prepared to give way.

(ii) The points on which he will wish to stand firm, in which case he should have his counter-arguments well prepared.

(c) Undecided. It will probably suffice to give a brief indication of what one's views are, while not pressing them on the other member, and to indicate what support they are likely to receive.

APPEARANCE

A psychological advantage may be obtained by having an appearance noticeably different from the rest of the group in some way which they are likely to admire and envy, e.g. by always sporting a rose in the button-hole! The Chairman may normally wish to underline his position of authority by being dressed rather more smartly than other members. On the other hand, if they all habitually wear conventionally smart clothes, this will be impossible and he may find it advantageous to dress differently, e.g. if he is a scientist to dress like a 'professor'.

TACTICS

The following examples of tactics vary from the wholly legitimate examples placed early in the list to those of more dubious morality placed later in the list. While these later tactics are not recommended except in self-defence, some people certainly employ them, and it is therefore desirable to recognize and guard against them so that these people do not obtain an unfair advantage.

Do not overdo The Hospitality (see overleaf)

(1) Master the papers beforehand, preferably not too long beforehand. Look up any relevant facts from the original source or as near to it as possible, and be prepared to quote both the facts and the source (e.g. the relevant section of an

Act, or the relevant paragraph of a book or report) in support of your argument.

(2) When the time and place of a meeting are being considered, try to stick to your home ground, while being accommodating about date and time of day.

(3) Make your guests comfortable and offer them sufficient hospitality to make them feel friendly disposed towards you. Do not overdo the hospitality, however, to such an extent that your guests will agree to things which they will later regret.

(4) If you are disagreeing with another member, build your argument on some point which he has made. Do not be obvious and say 'But you yourself said . . . ', but be more subtle and include your opponent's form of words in your own statement. This will make it seem to him familiar and perhaps more acceptable.

(5) It sometimes pays to flatter, though here again the references should be oblique and not too obvious.

(6) At a meeting, be prepared to go on as long as is necessary to gain your point, letting the other side get exhausted first.

(7) If an opponent has a bad argument, let him talk about it as much as he likes, so that you will have more weak points to demolish.

(8) Take advantage of likely exhaustion, and introduce the topic on which you particularly want agreement when people are too tired to argue but have just enough time to consider it before they disperse to catch trains, etc.

(9) Never overstate your case. When opposition is likely, spike your opponent's guns by conceding his main points (these can with advantage be overstated slightly, so that he himself is forced to withdraw somewhat in order to avoid looking ridiculous) but suggesting (not necessarily stating) that there are counters to them. If possible, keep one argument in reserve, to produce with telling effect when apparent deadlock has been reached.

(10) It sometimes pays to say 'to be quite frank . . . ' or 'speaking bluntly . . . ', while remaining as polite as possible. This may induce the other side to place *their* cards on the table.

(11) If the difficulties are practical, stress the point of principle. If they are theoretical, stress that you are a practical man.

(12) Where a compromise seems inevitable, start from an extreme position, so that you have maximum room for manoeuvre.

(13) Concede nothing until you have to and then make full play with the fact that you have made a concession and expect one in return.

If you are supporting the weakest party in a three-cornered vote, the best chance of success is to induce the two bigger parties to vote against each other first. Then if neither party wins a majority, your proposition or your candidate may eventually be adopted *faute de mieux*.

CO-OPERATION WITH COLLEAGUES

A final piece of advice, based on observations of people with high intelligence and strong personalities who have learned to make the most effective use of committees on which they have served: if you are the dominant member of a committee (especially if you are not the Chairman) it is essential that you should avoid making this fact too obvious. If you are wise, therefore, you will go out of your way to invite the co-operation of other members and to let them have as much credit as possible for what they do.

In particular:

(a) Develop your successive ideas, as far as possible in association with each other member of the committee in turn, and let each idea be credited to the pair of you, not just to you alone. Your ideas may well be improved by your colleague's comments but, even if they are not, to seek co-operation in this way makes for increased friendliness.

(b) When you have developed an idea in partnership with a colleague, invite him to present the actual proposal, then support it yourself.

(c) When quoting a good point made at a past meeting, attribute it to the appropriate committee member by name, even if the point was partly your own.

Ready appreciation of past contributions by your colleagues is likely to encourage their maximum co-operation in future.

9

THE SECRETARY'S DUTIES

'And so while the great ones depart to their dinner,
The secretary stays, growing thinner and thinner,
Racking his brain to record and report
What he thinks that they think that they ought to have thought.'[1]

IMPORTANCE OF THE SECRETARY'S ROLE

It is customary for any committee at intervals, sometimes at rather long intervals, to express appreciation of the services of their Secretary. With an Ad hoc Committee which presents a report, it is natural that the Secretary should include in the report (at the explicit direction of the committee) a graceful tribute to his services in drafting it. With a Standing Committee, a convenient opportunity to register thanks comes at the Annual General Meeting or other yearly meeting, and the thanks are likely to be especially profuse if there is thought to be any risk that the Secretary may resign and be difficult to replace. On such occasions there is ready and genuine appreciation of the sheer volume of work involved in preparing minutes and dealing with correspondence. There may also be tributes (their sincerity depending upon the actual drafting ability of the Secretary) to his skill in handling the paper work. These drafting duties are indeed important and will be discussed in Chapter 10. However, the Secretary of a committee is, or should be, much more than a note-taker, and it is doubtful whether there is sufficient appreciation of the part played by him in less obvious but equally important ways.

A Secretary's duties can be considered under three broad headings. First, it is his duty to make all arrangements for a committee meeting so as to give the greatest chance that the meeting will proceed efficiently and smoothly. This duty includes:

[1] Lines attributed to a 'versifying official' and quoted in The Turn of the Tide by Sir Arthur Bryant.

(1) Fixing the date and time of the next meeting so as to suit the convenience of as many members as possible. If the members are busy people, their other commitments are liable to intervene suddenly, in which case the Secretary will often have to alter the provisional arrangements for the meeting at short notice by means of an interlocking series of telephone calls.

(2) The Secretary must keep a watching brief on behalf of any committee member who is not present but is known to have strong views on an item (possibly obtaining a statement of them before the meeting).

(3) He is responsible for all physical arrangements for a meeting, including booking a suitable room and ensuring that members, especially those coming from a distance, can find it or are directed to it. The size of the room presents an interesting problem in applied psychology. On balance, there is probably advantage in having slightly more room than the committee needs, giving each member ample space to spread his papers, etc. This is in contrast to a public meeting where the ideal is to have the room slightly over-full, thereby assisting the impression that the meeting is popular and worth coming to.

(4) Ventilation deserves a heading to itself, since this aspect is both important and commonly neglected. For comfort, a committee room should be adequately warm, but it is imperative that it should be properly ventilated, or after an hour or so heads will begin to nod and attention wander. The Secretary will have a greater chance of pleasing most people if he ensures that windows are opened at the top rather than at the bottom (even though the top windows may be more difficult to get at) and on the same side of a room (preferably not the side overlooking a busy street) rather than on opposite sides.

(5) An important duty is to issue the agenda for the next meeting, having fixed the number of items and the order in which they should be taken. Very often the Secretary will wish to consult the Chairman about this and perhaps also discuss with him the approximate time that can be devoted to each item without falling behind with the business. Plan-

Ventilation is Most Important

ning a rough timetable in this way was discussed under the Chairman's duties in Chapter 6. Especially with a Standing Committee, at least half of the meeting is liable to be taken up with reading the minutes of the last meeting and discussing matters arising therefrom, with the result that later items on the agenda are either rushed or not reached. There is advantage therefore in varying the order. Sometimes, if there is one item of outstanding importance, this can be placed first on the agenda, before 'matters arising'. On another occasion, 'any other business' could be taken early, so that members can mention matters which otherwise they might never have a chance to raise.

(6) The Secretary can help members of a committee to get to know each other by e.g. arranging for them to meet at lunch or on other social occasions, and in the case of members who have not met before by mentioning common interests when introducing them. If a committee meeting is to have sessions

in the morning and afternoon, then it is helpful for the Secretary to arrange a communal lunch. This avoids the separation of the sexes or the formation of cliques, and in particular it helps to prevent certain members from going to ground in their clubs and returning late for the afternoon session.

(7) It is bad to circulate too much paper, but the Secretary can sometimes help, e.g. to avoid a deadlock by putting a suitable paper in at the right moment. The timing of papers can be important.

(8) By synthesizing policy statements or providing a summary of evidence, the Secretary can produce a basis for a report, can indicate the areas of agreement and can help to focus discussion on the remaining issues that have to be freed. In short, he can be a real steering force in the committee.

Second, during a meeting, the Secretary has to act as understudy to the Chairman, in:

(1) Seeing that each contribution by a member is understood. In the last resort, if it clearly is not understood, the Secretary may himself have to ask a question to clarify the point.

(2) Ensuring that the committee's view on each item is made clear before passing on to the next item. Here it is certainly for the Secretary to speak up and request precise instructions if he is not clear what has been agreed (or to nudge the Chairman and ask him to do this).

The Secretary may also:

(3) Have to assist the Chairman, between meetings, in talking to the other members and resolving any unnecessary doubts and worries. The Chairman and Secretary between them must make it clear to the other members that they are impartial and fair-minded, taking due account of all points and striving to ascertain the group view, and they may on occasions have to discourage other members from nobbling each other.

Finally, in preparing minutes or a report, the Secretary has to exercise, not only skill in drafting, but also judgment.

For example:

(1) Committees often reach conclusions by irrational means, out of mistaken loyalty, or in pique, or exasperation. If so, the Secretary has to endeavour to rationalize their views or, if this proves impossible, to give them a chance to alter their conclusion.

(2) In order to keep the minutes or report reasonably concise, the Secretary has to exercise discretion as to what to put in or leave out.

BRIEF FOR A MEETING

The Chairman will usually require a brief, and very often it is one of the Secretary's duties to prepare it for him. If so,

(1) His aim should be to make the brief as complete and self-contained as possible (with relevant papers in the files clearly tagged), so that the Chairman could at a pinch attend the meeting with no preparation other than a quick glance through the brief. (In practice of course the Chairman will wish to do a good deal more preparation than that.)

(2) The first part of the brief should be factual, with a summary of the historical or geographical facts of the case, a note of the points for discussion, and a list of the arguments for and against any proposals that have been put forward.

(3) The brief should contain also a commentary on the facts, e.g.:

    (a) Relative weight of opinion thought to be behind different points of view;

    (b) Comments on alternative proposals, and one's own recommendations;

    (c) Estimate of practical target date for project; and

    (d) Suggestions for preliminary or interim measures.

(4) The brief for a Chairman should suggest headings for discussion at the meeting and the order in which they might be taken.

(5) Where something is known about the people coming to the meeting, the brief might also advise on tactics at the meeting, e.g.:

(*a*) Order in which people might be invited to speak; and

(*b*) Means of persuading likely opponents of one's own recommendation to suggest constructive alternatives or else acquiesce in one's own proposals.

DUTIES AT AND AFTER A MEETING

At a committee meeting, the Secretary must make sure that he knows what decision has been reached on an item before the next one is taken. He should make full notes, but demands for a verbatim report may indicate that the group spirit is poor and that members no longer trust each other.

After the meeting, he should issue the minutes and consequential instructions, usually as soon as possible. Alternatively, the minutes can be sent out with the agenda for the next meeting or read out aloud at the next meeting.

10

MINUTES AND REPORTS

Minutes are always necessary to confirm what was agreed at a meeting. Without agreed minutes, different people's recollections of what transpired are bound to differ, and they are likely to differ increasingly with the passage of time, thus allowing occasion for misunderstanding and recrimination. The fullness of the minutes will depend upon the kind of committee and upon the nature of each item. If the committee is large, with the probability that several members are missing from each meeting, full minutes help these members to keep in touch with developments at the meeting they missed. If a decision is irreversible, e.g. the decision to send a letter of protest to somebody, then action of a self-explanatory kind is likely to stem from that decision, and there is less need to record the reasons behind it. If a decision is reversible, e.g. the decision to defer sending a letter of protest for the time being, there is more need to record the reasons behind it, for reference if the item comes up again at a later meeting. In any case, however, the Secretary will be wise to make full rough notes of the discussion and to keep them for reference until the minutes have been cleared.

The Secretary should dictate or write the minutes or at least his first draft of them, as soon as possible, before his memory starts to fade. If he waits (say) forty-eight hours until he is feeling fresher, he may find that the minutes flow more easily, but they are likely to be less accurate, as memory is often a selective process. The Quaker practice, by which the Clerk to a meeting drafts a note on each item and secures the agreement of the meeting to it before proceeding to the next item, has much to commend it.

In general, the Secretary probably supports the cohesion of a committee by stressing points of agreement. He should not gloss over objectives or points of disagreement that were made strongly or persisted with, but he can sometimes tone them down. For example, for 'Nonsense! I have never heard such a fatuous proposal', it may be desirable to substitute 'Mr Brown said that he could not support this proposal, since . . . ' The Secretary should avoid giving offence, and should e.g. make each reported utterance as clear and sensible as possible (however fully or vaguely it was in fact made at the meeting).

The points about a particular topic that are worth recording in the minutes should preferably be arranged in logical order, not necessarily the order in which they happened to be made. If there is advantage in inserting in the minutes something not said at the meeting, this should be done by means of a footnote, e.g. 'It was subsequently decided that this letter of enquiry need not be sent, since an adequate explanation had now been received'.

A wise Secretary will seek to avoid recording in the minutes an expression of views of a general kind (as opposed to a decision on a current topic) that is intended to bind the Committee's successors who, he may think, would not wish to be bound in this way. There is an analogy here with the Victorian patriarch who relished making a complicated will, leaving his money to his children, grandchildren and their heirs under complicated conditions limiting their freedom to spend the money as they wish. Similarly a committee which has considered a subject at length may feel that it has formed views which are valid for all time, e.g. that Conscription is good—or bad—for the youth of the country, not realizing that against a different background different considerations might seem decisive.

In general, it is simplest and best to record the gist of a discussion anonymously, without necessarily recording how much support each point of view obtained (which may be difficult to judge), saying 'The following points were made . . . ' In some contexts, e.g. when one member put a point very strongly, it may be preferable to attribute each remark to some one or more persons. If individuals are named, it is desirable not to overlook any contributor.

Finally, a point of detail can be mentioned about which

some people feel strongly. In minutes the Secretary should be consistent in his use of the present or past tense—the past tense is generally preferable.

TREATMENT OF MINUTES

There are three ways in which the minutes of a meeting are commonly presented to committee members:

(1) Written minutes are issued to all members soon after the meeting.

(2) Written minutes are issued to all members with the agenda for the next meeting; this can be a long time after the previous meeting took place.

(3) The minutes are read out aloud at the start of the next committee meeting. Normally, the Chairman then invites any comments on the minutes from those present. If the Quaker practice were followed of securing an agreed note on each item before proceeding to the next, the minutes would have been agreed at the previous meeting, and the reading of them out aloud would be to acquaint members not then present with what had transpired and to refresh the memories of the other members.

Method (1) has the advantage to members that they can read the minutes while the subject matter is still fresh in their minds. There is the possible disadvantage, however, that this may lead them to make numerous comments on the minutes, some contradictory, which it may be difficult for the Secretary to resolve to everyone's satisfaction. If there is some delay in issuing minutes, members are likely to have forgotten some of their minor worries before the minutes reach them.

Opinions differ on whether it should be necessary to circulate a draft note of a meeting, for comment and suggested amendments, to all who attended, or should have attended it. In general, this should not be necessary, and if written minutes are issued, they can be regarded as final subject to:

(a) Issue of a written corrigendum on any error of fact.

(b) Giving members an opportunity to raise queries on the

minutes at the next meeting. They can then be taken as read subject to any amendment proposed and carried on the spot.

If, however, a substantial part of the note of a meeting constitutes the draft of a section of the committee's report, then the precise wording is of importance, and it may be desirable to give an opportunity before the next meeting to suggest written amendments to the draft.

PREPARATION OF REPORTS

When a report is required, it facilitates its preparation if there is sufficient interval between successive meetings to allow time to draft those sections of the report covering points agreed at the last meeting. Points not yet agreed can be indicated for consideration at the next meeting.

Committees cannot draft. The Chairman has a special responsibility for distinguishing between points of substance and purely 'drafting points', i.e. points of style when the intended meaning is agreed. With regard to points of substance, each member of the committee should have the opportunity to comment, at every stage. Drafting points should be considered by the Chairman and Secretary together or by a drafting sub-committee of not more than three members. To ensure consistency of style and content, the final report should as far as possible be the work of one hand. It follows that it is a waste of time to start to draft any section of a report in its final form until all points of substance have been agreed.

When a draft paper has to be revised, if there is a point of substance, preferably the author of the draft should note the point and amend the draft himself. If he is not sure that he has grasped the point completely or if he finds it a difficult point to incorporate, he can ask his colleague who raised the point to help with a counterdraft, which he can then amend himself. Purely drafting points should be left to a single person to settle who is an expert in English, not necessarily the originator of the paper.

11

SUMMARY OF FACTORS MAKING FOR THE SUCCESS OR FAILURE OF A COMMITTEE

Committees are an indispensable part of the democratic way of life. Their use can, however, be abused, e.g. to give the illusion of general agreement to a decision already taken by an individual, or as a means of shelving decision on an awkward problem. And they can be miserably inefficient. For a committee to do its job well and serve a useful purpose, the circumstances of its constitution must be appropriate and the committee must be technically competent.

By appropriate circumstances is meant:

(1) The committee is given clear terms of reference defining topics which are within its competence to consider, with a view to agreed recommendations or decisions.

(2) On these topics sufficient information has been assembled to enable an informed discussion to take place.

(3) There is time enough to enable adequate discussion by the committee before decisions have to be reached.

Points (2) and (3) together imply correct timing of items coming before the committee. They must not come up so early that the basic information is lacking or so late that the relevant decisions have already been taken elsewhere.

By technical competence is meant:

(1) The committee is clear as to its purpose and powers, and consists of people who are suitable to its terms of reference.

(2) While being able to consider all relevant points of view, it is small enough to make informal discussion possible.

(3) The Chairman is determined to make the committee work well and is the right kind of person to do this. This means that he studies other people's qualifications and feelings and tries to draw from each member the best contribution that he can make. The Chairman is willing to take advice but at the same time able to summarize the group views as they develop and to guide the committee towards reaching group decisions.

(4) Other members should preferably have achieved some competence at committee work either by training or by practical experience under skilled Chairmen—experience under a variety of unskilled Chairmen may be worse than useless.

(5) The committee is serviced by an efficient Secretary. In addition to making an accurate note of the meetings, he helps members to get to know each other and to study matters likely to come up at future meetings; and he sees that all decisions or recommendations of the committee are correctly represented to people outside the committee, so that appropriate action can be taken.

If the above conditions are fulfilled, a committee should be successful in three ways:

(1) Business is got through with reasonable despatch, and matters once settled are not raised again.

(2) There is general satisfaction with group decisions and conviction that, though not necessarily perfect, they are the best decisions that could have been reached in the circumstances.

(3) Members find meetings on the whole interesting and enjoyable, and each member feels that he is contributing by his presence. If over a prolonged period he does not feel this, he should consider how he could make some useful contribution—or resign from the committee.

APPENDIX—SPECIMEN COMMITTEE MEETING

This chapter presents three successive accounts of an imaginary committee meeting, which will be called meetings A, B and C, with a commentary in each case on how the meeting is handled. The meeting is called by the Chairman of the local residents' association to discuss proposals for an Ashstone by-pass. Ashstone is supposed to be a town with some 20,000 inhabitants situated about 15 miles from London on the main road to Eastport. Traffic passing through the town causes a great deal of congestion, particularly at weekends, and already before the war there were proposals to build a by-pass avoiding all built-up areas. With the hold-up in new road construction during and after the war these plans were shelved, but they have recently been revived, and it is regarded as probable that some kind of by-pass is contemplated. The Chairman of the Ashstone residents' association has therefore called a committee meeting to test the reaction of various interested parties and to formulate proposals, on what the attitude of the association should be. Similar situations have no doubt arisen in real life from proposals to build a by-pass, but both the places and the characters described in this chapter are of course wholly fictitious.

The people attending the committee meeting are:

Chairman of the Ashstone residents' association	Mr Makepeace
Vice-Chairman of the Association	Mr Davis
Secretary of the Association (and of the meeting)	Mr Jones
Another member of the Association	Mr Brown
Secretary of the Ashstone road safety committee	Miss Ingram
Secretary of the Ashstone Chamber of Commerce	Mr Spenser
Owner of the Paragon garage on the Eastport road near the centre of Ashstone	Mr Magneto
Proprietor of the Red Lion Hotel, Ashstone	Mr Andrew
Prominent business man and resident of Loamhurst (a village within the Ashstone Urban District but distinct from Ashstone town)	Mr Goldrib
Another resident of Loamhurst	Mr Jenkins
Owner of a farm near Loamhurst	Mr Greenstick
Area Secretary of the Society for the Preservation of Rural England	Miss Tweedyman
Area Secretary of the Motorists' Club	Mr Royce

Chairman's Brief for the Meeting

Before the meeting the Chairman had a preliminary discussion with the Vice-Chairman and Secretary who helped him to prepare the following brief. Up to the final section on 'tactics' the briefs for the three meetings were identical.

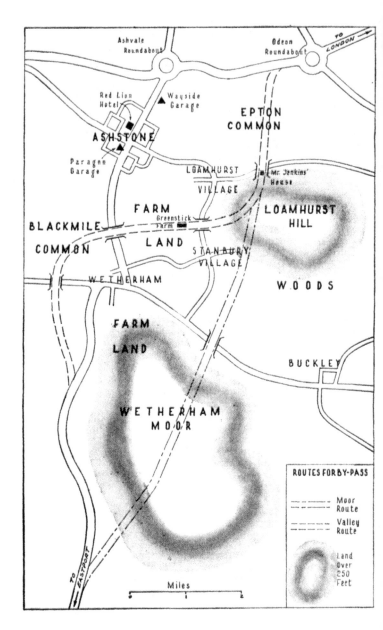

TO LONDON

Ashvale
Roundabout

Odeon
Roundabout

Red Lion
Hotel

Wayside
Garage

EPTON
COMMON

ASHSTONE

Paragon
Garage

LOAMHURST

Mr. Jenkins'
House

VILLAGE

LOAMHURST
HILL

FARM

Greenstick
Farm

BLACKMILE

LAND

STANBURY
VILLAGE

COMMON

WETHERHAM

WOODS

BUCKLEY

FARM

LAND

WETHERHAM
MOOR

TO EASTPORT

ROUTES FOR BY-PASS

- - - - - Moor
Route

- · - · - Valley
Route

Land
Over
250
Feet

Miles

0   1   2

(A) *Facts*

Main arguments for an Ashstone by-pass are:

  (1) Save delay to through traffic.

  (2) Reduce road casualties.

  (3) Reduce congestion in Ashstone and Wetherham.

  (4) Provide better communications for Loamhurst (Chairman's marginal note—a dubious argument).

  (5) A by-pass will have to be built one day. The sooner it is built, the smaller the damage to property, amenities, etc.

Main arguments against are:

  (1) Very expensive.

  (2) New road would destroy rural amenities.

  (3) And use up valuable agricultural land.

  (4) There might be fresh ribbon development (though surely this could be avoided).

  (5) Some 12 houses, 8 of them new, would have to be demolished if the valley route were followed.

  (6) Harm to some commercial interests.

  (7) Hardship to certain individuals.

  (8) Chance that the road traffic through Ashstone might be reduced, e.g. by a fall in population or in the number of cars (this seems most unlikely).

(B) *Comments on Facts*

(1) Great weight of opinion that traffic congestion in Ashstone and Wetherham must be reduced. Objections from Loamhurst represent only a minority of the whole association but a majority in Loamhurst itself, and their point of view must be considered.

(2) A by-pass is probably inevitable, but route not decided. We can express views on this.

(3) Realistic starting date is some 3-10 years from now, and we can decide whether or not to press for the earlier date.

(C) *Headings for Discussion*

(1) Factual statements about the traffic situation in Ashstone by Mr Royce and Miss Ingram, followed by comments thereon.

(2) Assuming it is agreed that some action is necessary, we can consider in turn:

  (a) palliatives, such as speed limits and footbridges.

  (b) widening the main road through Ashstone.

  (c) a by-pass following the 'valley route'.

  (d) alternative routes, if any.

(3) If we decide to support a by-pass, we should consider what starting date is likely to be practicable, and also interim measures such as:

  (a) sterilize agreed route,

  (b) improvements to existing main road,

(c) other road safety measures,

(d) means of compensation to parties adversely affected by the proposals.

(4) Decide what action the Association should take to secure implementation of our proposals.

[Comment: So far the brief, which is intended to seem a reasonable one, is common to all three versions of the committee meeting. The final section on tactics, however, differs according to the temperament and personality of the three imaginary Chairmen.]

(D) Handling the Meeting — Tactics

MEETING A	MEETING B	MEETING C
(1) 'There are likely to be strongly conflicting views from different parties, and it will be essential to give everyone a fair chance to express his own point of view.	(1) 'There are likely to be strongly conflicting views from different parties, and it may not be possible to reach unanimous agreement. After hearing different points of view, therefore, it will be up to me to give a lead in order to influence the meeting to agree on what seems on balance the best solution.	(1) 'This problem inevitably involves conflicting interests and I must allow each member a fair chance to express his point of view. In order to stand any chance of reaching general agreement, I must try to keep the discussion on the right lines, drawing attention wherever possible to points of agreement and common interest.
(2) A decision by a narrow majority on what course we favour would have the unfortunate effect of hardening opinion on both sides, possibly even of splitting the Association. It would be better, if necessary, to postpone a decision, with the chance that the development of events will operate towards reaching general agreement.	(2) To prevent the meeting lasting too long and to avoid sterile controversies, I must be quick to intervene as necessary to keep the discussion on the right lines and prevent people from pursuing irrelevant issues.	(2) The best chance of agreement might lie in a modification of the valley route with less damage to farmland and rural amenities, and I must try to allow members to think constructively along these lines before their opinions become hardened.

96

| (3) I must remain strictly neutral.' | (3) If the Association is to exert any influence on events, it must reach some decision and make its views known in the right quarters.' | (3) If the Association can reach general agreement, it should be able to exert influence by making its views known in the right quarters.' |

[*Comment*: These final notes on tactics show Chairman A to be a fair-minded, cautious person, content to hold the ring, but not prepared to play an active part in guiding the meeting towards an agreed solution.

Chairman B is determined to make speakers stick to the point in order to get through the business in one meeting and reach definite decisions, even if they are not unanimous ones.

Chairman C also hopes that the committee will reach a solution, but feels it important that it should be a generally agreed one, and is looking actively for some means of reconciling opposing points of view.]

Statement of the Purpose of the Meeting

This is common to meetings A, B and C.

(1) The Chairman. 'Good evening ladies and gentlemen. The purpose of this meeting, as you know, is to consider the proposals for an Ashstone by-pass, to discuss what our attitude should be and, if possible, to agree on some definite plan and decide what action the Association should take to implement it. Before we consider the various possibilities, I think we should start with an objective review of the facts about the traffic situation in Ashstone, and I therefore call upon Mr Royce, the Area Secretary of the Motorists' Club, to make a statement.'

[*Comment*: The Chairman's introductory remarks should be as brief as possible. If he himself talks at any length, this will make it more difficult for him to request other members of the committee to speak briefly later. At the same time, it is appreciated that on occasion it would be tactful for him, for example, to extend a special welcome to someone who had been absent, ill or who did not normally attend meetings of the committee.]

Description of the Traffic Situation in Ashstone

(2) Mr Royce. 'Thank you, Mr Chairman, ladies and gentlemen. As you no doubt know from personal experience, all the traffic from London to Barchester, Eastport and beyond has to travel along the Eastport road through Ashstone. Ashstone is now a heavily built-up area, and there are bottlenecks caused by the traffic lights in the middle of the town, by the four pedestrian crossings and by the minor intersecting roads. The traffic congestion is always bad but at weekends it becomes intolerable. On Sunday evenings it is common for queues a mile long to form, and traffic may well take twenty minutes to pass through Ashstone. Apart from the waste of time and money, the lengthy delay naturally frays the temper of motorists

and perhaps tempts them to take unnecessary risks in trying to make up for lost time. The traffic congestion in Wetherham, three miles further along the Eastport road, is only slightly less bad than in Ashstone, and matters are made worse by the right angle bend in the middle of the town with the main road from Buckley coming in on the left-hand side. A new road by-passing Ashstone and Wetherham would shorten the journey by at least half an hour and relieve the congestion in the towns. Already before the war there were plans to build a by-pass, following the so-called "valley route" round the east and south of Loamhurst and skirting Stanbury on the north. This route would at that date have passed through open country. Unfortunately since the war this route has been partly built on, so that a number of houses would have to be demolished. Now that an extensive national programme of new road construction has at last got under way, I understand that the proposals for an Ashstone by-pass have been revived in the Ministry of Transport, who would be willing to give the scheme fairly high priority, especially if it were agreed locally that the scheme would be in the general interest.'

(3) The Chairman. 'Thank you, Mr Royce. Miss Ingram.'

(4) Miss Ingram. 'I have already distributed a memorandum (this is reproduced as an Annex) setting out the numbers of people killed and injured on the main road through Ashstone during the first six months of this year, classified according to type of road user. These figures prove the existing road to be a most dangerous one, for motorists, cyclists and pedestrians alike; and they show the need for a by-pass, which would certainly cut the casualties, especially among cyclists and pedestrians, who could cycle to and from school and do their shopping in Ashstone in comparative peace.'

Discussion of the Traffic Problems in Ashstone

(5) Mr Andrew. 'I understand these arguments, of course, but I should like to draw attention to the very serious effect that a diversion of the main road would have on any business such as mine. There is very little demand for meals out from the local residents, and at least nine-tenths of the trade of my hotel comes from passing motorists. If the bulk of these motorists were diverted to another route by-passing Ashstone, there would be a catastrophic drop in custom and my hotel would probably have to close down, with a consequential loss of amenity to those residents who do like to dine out in comfort. I may say that Mr Smith, the proprietor of the Wayside garage on the northern outskirts of Ashstone, feels exactly as I do about this threat to our living, and I have no doubt that many owners of shops along the Eastport road through Ashstone will take the same line. Is a by-pass really necessary? We have heard, for example, that in Wetherham congestion is caused largely by the right-angle bend in the middle of the town. If this were straightened out, the traffic could flow faster.'

(6) Mr Spenser. 'As Secretary of the Ashstone Chamber of Commerce, I may say that, while I sympathize with Mr Andrew's point of view, it is

not generally shared by other local traders. The through traffic from London to Barchester and Eastport is not interested in shopping in Ashstone but wants to pass through as quickly as possible. Nothing would be lost, therefore, if this traffic were diverted to a by-pass. On the other hand, many people living in the neighbourhood who want to shop in Ashstone are put off by the congestion and by the difficulty of parking, and some of them may be forced to shop elsewhere. I think Mr Andrew may be taking too gloomy a view of his own situation, and he might succeed in attracting new custom from the people who would come to shop in Ashstone if they could do so in peace and comfort. As regards the possible road straightening in Wetherham, there would certainly be objections from the three or four tradespeople whose premises would have to be demolished, probably without really having much effect on the congestion, and in any case no such improvement could be made in Ashstone, where the main road is already pretty straight. On balance, it is clear that something drastic needs to be done.'

(7) Mr Magneto. 'I agree. While passing motorists may want to stop for petrol, the existing congestion is such that they may not be able to do so without obstructing the main road. This certainly applies to my own garage near the centre of Ashstone.'

(8) The Chairman. 'Thank you, gentlemen. Any other views, please?'

(9) Mr Goldrib. 'The traffic situation in Ashstone is certainly very bad, and so it is in the whole district. We need new roads to improve communications between Loamhurst and London.'

MEETING A	MEETINGS B AND C
(10) Mr. Greenstick. 'But any new roads round Loamhurst would waste much valuable agricultural land. Why should the farmers always have to suffer, and our food production be cut regardless, and our countryside spoilt? And if any houses have to be knocked down to make room for more cars, why should this always be done in the country rather than in the towns?'	(10) Mr Greenstick. 'But any new roads round Loamhurst would waste much valuable agricultural land.' (11) The Chairman. 'Yes, Mr Greenstick, we will come to that point later when we discuss specific proposals.'

[Comment: Chairman A ought not to have allowed Mr Greenstick to start an argument about spoiling farmland and the countryside at this stage when the meeting was discussing the facts about traffic congestion in Ashstone.

Chairmen B and C were right to intervene in the way they did. Mr Greenstick was content to keep quiet for the moment and wait to make his point later in the meeting. Items 11 and 12 in version A, which are irrelevant, are thus avoided at meetings B and C.]

(11) Mr Goldrib. 'It is generally more efficient to import food from countries where they can farm on a big scale. We must remember too that 90 per cent of us in Britain live in towns and are not greatly concerned with the countryside.'

(12) Miss Tweedyman. 'Then you ought to be!'

(13) The Chairman. 'There are clearly two points of view on this, but we mustn't waste time arguing. Most of us seem to think that the traffic congestion in Ashstone is serious, and that the situation is likely to get worse unless we do something about it. The question is, what?'

(11 *cont.*) The Chairman. 'It has been established that the traffic congestion in Ashstone is serious, and the situation seems likely to get worse unless we find a cure.'

All three meetings then continue as follows:

(13 *cont.*) The Chairman. 'I suggest that there are four possibilities which we might consider in turn:

(a) The pre-war scheme of a by-pass following the commons route.
(b) Measures other than new road construction, such as speed limits and footbridges for pedestrians.
(c) Widening the main road through Ashstone.
(d) Alternative routes for a by-pass, if any.

Let us consider first what could be done by measures other than new road construction.'

Discussion of Measures other than New Road Construction

(14) Mr Jenkins. 'It is well worth considering first what improvements could be made by such means, before we go on to discuss schemes for a by-pass which, whatever advantages it might bring, would do much harm to the peaceful village of Loamhurst. We have been told of the high proportion of accidents, especially to motor cyclists and cyclists, on the section of the main road between the Odeon and Ashvale roundabouts which, though winding and only three-lane, is derestricted. Here a 40 m.p.h. speed limit should cut accidents without materially slowing up the traffic. Possibly within Ashstone itself the speed limit should be 20 or even 15 m.p.h. On the other hand, in the centre of Ashstone, which is the worst bottleneck, the flow of traffic could be improved by providing footbridges or subways for pedestrians to cross the main road. What do you think, Miss Ingram?'

(15) Miss Ingram. 'I agree that these measures might avert some accidents and to that extent they would do good, but of course there would be disadvantages, and I fear that any plan which allowed an increasing mass of traffic to pass through Ashstone would leave a serious road safety problem.'

(16) Mr Goldrib. 'On our main roads the need is to speed up traffic, not slow it down. Experience has shown that, even when footbridges are provided, the public won't use them.'

(17) Mr Spenser. 'Imposition of speed limits without diverting any traffic could only make the congestion worse. Footbridges in the centre of Ashstone would be most unsightly and destroy the character of the town.'

(18) Mr Davis. 'Footbridges are no use for prams, so their use could not be made compulsory. Prams could negotiate tunnels with inclined ramps, but these take up a lot of space, and I doubt whether there would be room for them in the centre of Ashstone. In any case, these measures would not constitute a long-term solution.'

MEETING A

(19) The Chairman. 'Any other views?'

[Comment: This question by the Chairman was superfluous, since Mr Davis had just summed up the position re footbridges very well. The very general wording 'Any other views?', not directed to a specific issue, also gave a second opportunity to Mr Greenstick to air his grievance about the country being done down relative to towns. The Chairman would have done better to have taken the opportunity provided by Mr Davis's summing up of moving smoothly on to the next point.]

(20) Mr Greenstick. 'Why should footbridges or tunnels be regarded as more unsightly or more of a nuisance in towns than in the country? We farmers already have to put up with them wherever railways cross our land, and we would have to put up with many more of them spoiling our farms if a new by-pass were built.'

(21) Mr Magneto. 'More people live in towns. Also there is more countryside to spoil, so it matters less there.'

(22) The Chairman. 'I don't think we need go into that. We don't seem to agree on the desirability of footbridges or tunnels, so let's pass on to the other three possibilities.

MEETINGS B AND C

(19) The Chairman. 'Clearly, as Mr Davis points out, these would be only temporary expedients. We must try to agree on some permanent solution to the problem.'

[Comment: The Chairman was again right to intervene in this way. Items 20 and 21 in version A, which are irrelevant, are thus avoided.]

All three meetings then continue as follows:

(22 cont.) The Chairman. 'The second suggestion I mentioned was to widen the main road through Ashstone.'

(23) Mr Greenstick. 'This would be better than wasting good agricultural land!'

(24) Mr Spenser. 'Any such scheme would mean either cutting the width of pavements, which are already too narrow for the comfort and safety of shoppers, or extensive demolition or setting back the frontages of property. This would be both highly inconvenient and very expensive in compensation.'

(25) Miss Tweedyman. 'We want to avoid spoiling the countryside, but neither do we want to demolish the houses in the centre of Ashstone, many of which are of considerable architectural interest and value.'

(26) Miss Ingram. 'If the main road were widened, it would become even more difficult and dangerous to cross.'

(27) Mr Brown. 'And make Ashstone even noisier to live in.'

<table>
<tr><td align="center">MEETING A</td><td align="center">MEETINGS B AND C</td></tr>
</table>

MEETING A	MEETINGS B AND C

(28) The Chairman. 'Any other views?'

[*Comment*: Again this unfortunate phrase—views on what? Mr Jenkins looks as if he would like to speak.]

(28 *cont.*) 'Mr Jenkins, would you like to say something?'

(29) Mr Jenkins. 'The ever-increasing noise from aeroplanes, motor bikes, transistor wireless sets, etc., is becoming quite intolerable. Nobody likes it but nobody has the courage to do anything about it. Let's keep our few remaining country villages quiet!'

(30) Mr Magneto: 'This is the inevitable price of progress.'

(31) The Chairman. 'This is all very interesting, but we had better get on. Most of us seem to think that by elimination some kind of a by-pass seems the only solution to the Ashstone traffic problem, provided of course that we can hit upon a route that would not have too many of the disadvantages that Mr Greenstick and Mr Jenkins have mentioned.'

(28) The Chairman. 'This suggestion would not really be practicable.'

[*Comment*: The Chairman was again right to sum up the general feeling, Items 29 and 30 in version A, which are irrelevant, are thus avoided.]

(31) The Chairman. 'Some kind of a by-pass seems the only solution to the Ashstone traffic problem, and it is up to us to decide which route would confer the greatest benefit and have fewest disadvantages.'

All three meetings continue as follows:

(31 *cont.*) The Chairman. 'Let us consider first the "valley route". Mr Davis, would you please describe the course that route would take, for the benefit of those of us who may not be completely familiar with this plan?'

Description of Valley Route for Ashstone By-Pass

(32) Mr Davis. 'The proposed new by-pass is shown in intermittent lines on this map. It would leave the existing main road shortly after the Odeon roundabout, pass round the east and south of Loamhurst, skirt Stanbury on the north, cross the existing main road at Blackmile Common, and skirt Wetherham on the north. The total length of the by-pass would be about $7\frac{1}{2}$ miles, compared with $6\frac{1}{2}$ miles of the existing main road.

The chief engineering problem would be the construction of a fairly deep cutting about half a mile long through the high ground in the vicinity of Wexley Hall to the east of Loamhurst. Viaducts would be required to carry the new road over the road across Epton Common, over the Ashstone to Stanbury road, and over the existing main roads across Blackmile Common. Apart from linking roads at these four points, no access whatever to the new road would be permitted. The road would for the most part be sunk slightly below the level of the surrounding land, and footbridges would be provided at intervals of half a mile or so to enable pedestrians to cross the road.

The new road would, for the first 2½ miles and last 2 miles pass through low lying commons and heaths, hence the name the "valley route", but for the middle 3 miles or so lying between Loamhurst and Stanbury the road would traverse farm land. The new by-pass would be double track, each track being a uniform 36 feet wide to take three lines of traffic. It is for consideration whether cycling tracks should be provided also. It would cost some £5-6 million.

The main arguments in favour of this scheme, as I see it, are:

(1) It would save delay to through traffic.

(2) It would reduce road casualties.

(3) It would reduce congestion in Ashstone and Wetherham.

The main arguments against the scheme are:

(1) There would be some destruction of rural amenities.

(2) It would use up some valuable agricultural land.

(3) Some 12 houses, mostly new ones, would have to be demolished.

On balance, I must admit I feel in favour of this scheme as following the best route that is practicable. A by-pass will have to be built one day and, the sooner it is built, the smaller the damage to property and amenities. Nor need the new road be a blot on the landscape any more than (say) the Winchester by-pass is ugly. When the Winchester by-pass was first proposed, there were storms of protest about spoiling St Catherine's hill, but in fact it is now generally agreed that the by-pass fits quite well into the landscape, and it has certainly saved the town from strangulation.'

(33) The Chairman. 'Thank you, Mr Davis, for your lucid exposition. Any other views?'

(34) Mr Jenkins. 'Notwithstanding Mr Davis's references to the Winchester by-pass, where the situation was quite different in that the land affected was only rough pasture, I must object to the valley route. It would have a disastrous effect on Loamhurst, and 12 houses, mostly new ones, would have to be demolished.'

(35) Mr Greenstick. 'As Mr Davis pointed out, the so-called valley route would for 3 miles go through good farm land, not only ruining much land, but dividing the farms in half and making what was left difficult to run. People still fail to realize the vital importance of our farms and their food production to Britain in wartime . . . '

MEETING A

[*Comment*: The Chairman would have been well advised to intervene before Mr Greenstick pursued this particular argument further and caused other members of the committee to ride their particular hobby horses.]

(35 *cont.*) Mr Greenstick. 'In peacetime it doesn't particularly matter if we have to import most of our food from abroad. But in wartime, when these supplies from overseas are liable to be cut off, every acre of good agricultural land under cultivation in Britain is of vital importance.'

(36) Miss Tweedyman. 'I fail to see the relevance of Mr Greenstick's last remarks. We are not planning for war ! But I agree that we shouldn't spoil what is left of our countryside with still more ribbon development.'

(37) Mr Magneto. 'That argument can be overdone. There are far too many tiresome planning restrictions that hold up progress. For example, my own garage premises are very cramped and I should like to extend them but I am not allowed to. The owner of the property on one side refuses to sell, and on the other side there is an old building scheduled as an ancient monument, and I have been refused permission to extend in that direction either.'

(38) Mr Spenser (annoyed by Mr Greenstick and Miss Tweedyman). 'A by-pass is essential. We have heard a lot about spoiling the countryside, where not many people want to go anyway. You can walk over the commons any day of the week and not meet more than a handful of people. Most residents would be better pleased if we developed a proper park and recreation ground in Ashstone itself.'

(39) Mr Goldrib (who also has been irked by Mr Greenstick and Miss Tweedyman). 'I agree that a by-pass is essential, and that not many of us are interested in country walks. And it can't be helped if a few houses have to be knocked down; they can be rebuilt elsewhere. In the interests of progress, someone has to suffer.'

(40) Mr Jenkins. 'But why us in Loamhurst? Keep the route away from Loamhurst within Ashstone, which is already to a large extent spoilt and noisy !'

(41) Miss Ingram. 'That would scarcely contribute to road safety.'

MEETINGS B AND C

(36) The Chairman. 'Yes, we take your point, Mr Greenstick, but you have already made clear your objections to the valley route, and we must consider all points of view. Can I have other views, please, on the valley route?'

[*Comment*: The Chairman was again right to intervene. Items 36, 37 and most of 38-40 in version A, which were irrelevant, are thus avoided.]

(37) Mr Spenser. 'A by-pass is essential and I consider the valley route a reasonable one.'

(38) Miss Ingram. 'I agree.'

(39) Mr Goldrib. 'And so do I.'

All three meetings continue as follows:

Discussion of Possible Shorter Route

(42) Miss Tweedyman. 'What about an alternative, shorter route for the by-pass?'

MEETINGS A AND B

MEETING C

(43) The Chairman. 'Right, let us consider the possibility of a shorter route and then compare the relative merits of the two schemes.'

[*Comment:* The Chairman is hoping that some kind of a compromise solution may emerge, but the wording of the above sentence is not helpful to this end, since attention is directed to these two schemes only.]

(43) The Chairman. 'Right, let us consider the possibility of a shorter route, and then compare the advantages and disadvantages of these routes and any other route that might prove practicable.' [*Comment:* By wording the above sentence as he did, the Chairman left the door open to any member of the committee to suggest an alternative solution if one occurred to him.]

All three meetings continue as follows:

(44) Mr Greenstick. 'Yes, why should not a shorter route be found? avoiding farmland and unspoilt countryside? After all, why should country people always be ignored and townsfolk have everything their own way?'

(45) The Chairman. 'Yes, I take your point, Mr Greenstick, but you have already made clear your objections to the valley route, and not everybody agrees with you. What sort of route should this shorter by-pass follow? Any suggestions?'

(46) Miss Tweedyman. 'I suggest we might consider an inner ring road, using existing side streets but rounding off all sharp corners to help traffic flow.'

(47) Mr. Spenser. 'But this would mean knocking down a lot of property in Ashstone, far more than in the valley route. Even with extensive demolitions to round off corners, this hotchpotch of narrow local roads would be quite inadequate to serve as an inner by-pass.'

MEETING A

[*Comment:* Mr Spenser has taken Miss Tweedyman's proposal to refer to a two-way by-pass, whereas probably she had in mind a one-way ring road, using the existing main road to carry traffic the other way. The Chairman should have intervened to clarify exactly what she was proposing.]

MEETINGS B AND C

(48) The Chairman. 'I think Miss Tweedyman had it in mind that the existing main road could be made one-way, as has been done in certain other towns, and the existing side streets, without extensive demolition, could be used to carry traffic one-way in the other direction.' (Miss Tweedyman nods her assent.)

[*Comment:* The Chairman was right

105

(48) Mr Davis. 'Furthermore, only trunk roads attract 100 per cent government grant. The cost of improving local roads would have to be met partly or largely from the local rates.'

to clarify Miss Tweedyman's suggestion, even though it does not seem a practicable one.]

(49) Mr Davis. 'I doubt whether the existing side streets would be adequate to carry all the through traffic even in one direction. Furthermore, only trunk roads attract 100 per cent government grant. The cost of improving local roads would have to be met partly or largely from the local rates.'

All three meetings continue as follows:

(50) Miss Ingram. 'These quiet residential roads would be entirely unsuited to carry a heavy stream of traffic and would become very difficult to cross. This would be bad for road safety.'

Interim Summing Up by Chairman

MEETING A	MEETING B	MEETING C
(51) The Chairman. 'Well, I feel we have had a useful discussion, and at least we know better other people's points of view. One or two people haven't said much. Mr Andrew?' [*Comment*: The meeting has made no progress, except that the more argumentative members have been hardened in their respective points of view. The Chairman decides to make one last attempt to obtain a new or compromise solution from one of the members who has not said much, but his choice of Mr Andrew is unfortunate. There was no reason to suppose that he would make any constructive contribution.] (52) Mr Andrew. 'Any	(51) The Chairman. 'It is clear that some members prefer the valley route and others would prefer a shorter route, some kind of an inner ring road. We have heard arguments from all interested parties. Let us consider the facts as objectively and impartially as possible and decide which solution we prefer. The valley route would certainly relieve congestion and help to reduce accidents. At present, therefore, it is the recommended route. However this road would be expensive, costing some £5-6 million, and would involve loss of agricultural land and some demolition. Because of	(51) The Chairman. 'It is clear that the valley route would relieve congestion and help to reduce accidents, which is why some members favour it. On the other hand, it would involve loss of agricultural land and some demolition, which is why other members object to it. Any shorter route would be bound to suffer from other serious disadvantages, as has been pointed out. Before continuing to discuss these proposals, I wonder if there is any other route that would both relieve congestion and confer the same

improvements have to be paid for, and you won't do that by killing the goose that lays the golden eggs. In other words, don't divert traffic from Ashstone and ruin the business of traders like Mr Smith and myself.'

(53) Miss Ingram. 'With respect, Mr Andrew, that is a selfish point of view. The by-pass is essential in the interests of road safety, whatever the cost and inconvenience to a few people. It is really only inconvenience, since there will be compensation of any traders who suffer business losses.'

(54) Mr Andrew. 'Cost matters too. We pay rates and you can't reduce revenue and increase expenditure without going bankrupt.'

(55) The Chairman. 'Obviously we don't all see eye-to-eye. Any other view? Mr Brown?' (Mr Brown was going to make a suggestion, but in view of the general discord, the hot reception afforded to Mr Andrew, and the references to high cost, his nerve fails him and he shakes his head.)

(55 cont.) 'I don't think we can reach a decision tonight. I suggest that we all think calmly for a month and discuss the matter again at our next meeting.'

these objections, it has been suggested that a shorter route might be found. This in turn would be bound to suffer from certain disadvantages. In order for it to constitute a broad reasonably straight by-pass, there would have to be extensive demolitions, which would be both costly and unsightly. If a mere one-way street system is contemplated by linking existing roads, such a route would be awkward to follow and probably more dangerous than the existing main road. In addition, part of the expenditure would have to be borne by the local rates. On the whole, therefore, I doubt whether a shorter route is practicable. Before I put the matter to the vote, are there any further comments?'

[Comment: The Chairman's summing up has done nothing to resolve the differences of opinion or to help arrive at a compromise or integrated solution acceptable to all. The references to being 'objective and impartial" would not cut much ice, and a mere recapitulation of argu-

benefits as the valley route and avoid some of the disadvantages of this route. Let's all think again quietly for a minute or two and see if anyone can come up with a fresh suggestion.'

[Comment: The Chairman's interim summing up has indicated that, while all members have made useful points, no solution so far put forward is wholly satisfactory. His suggestion of a short pause is helpful to anyone who has a fresh idea to put forward.]

ments would tend to
harden people's minds.
He is clearly resigned
to a majority decision
and has indicated
which way he himself
would vote.]

General Comment on Meeting A

The above record of meeting A is intended to be a realistic account of how
a meeting might go in the circumstances described, with various interests
represented by people with a normal mixture of selfishness and co-operativeness. The Chairman in version A was portrayed as an agreeable person,
well liked and respected by all members of the committee. He was determined to be impartial and to give everybody a fair chance to speak. Had
this not been manifestly the case, the meeting would have gone far worse,
with two or more people often speaking at once, and members saying
'Nonsense!' and being rude to each other. In that event, the meeting might
well have ended in a row, as sometimes happens in such circumstances in
real life. If the meeting had been less well prepared, time might also have
been wasted in arguments about the facts, e.g. about the percentage grant
payable by the central government on various types of road, or as to
whether the estimate of cost of a by-pass along the valley route was a
reasonable one. Nevertheless, the meeting ended inconclusively, without
any progress having been made, and must therefore be regarded as a
complete failure.

Meetings B and C continue with discussion of a new suggestion by
Mr Brown.

Discussion of Moors Route

After a pause, (52) Mr Brown. 'Might I suggest a solution?'

(53) The Chairman. 'Please do!'

(54) Mr Brown. 'I wonder if we could consider the possibility of the
by-pass following a different, longer route, keeping on the eastern fringe
of the Ashstone urban district. It could follow the valley route for the
first 2½ miles, but then instead of turning west between Loamhurst and
Stanbury it could continue to the east and south of Stanbury and then
more or less in a straight line to the east and south of Wetherham, rejoin-
ing the main Eastport road some 5 miles south of Wetherham. This by-pass
would be longer than the valley route, about 10½ miles instead of 7½,
but it would follow a more direct route and save through traffic from
London to Eastport about 2 miles. The road would go almost entirely
through woods or moors and would avoid the good farmland between
Loamhurst and Stanbury, including Mr Greenstick's farm. Also fewer
houses would have to be demolished.'

(55) Mr Jenkins. 'Would my house be spared?'

(56) Mr Brown. 'I'm afraid not.'

(57) Mr Jenkins. 'Then, I don't like it any better than the valley route.'

(58) Mr Spenser. 'It sounds a sensible suggestion, but what about the cost?'

(59) Mr Brown. 'Because the route would be longer, I'm afraid it would certainly cost more than the valley route.'

(60) The Chairman. 'How much more, I wonder? What would you say, Mr Royce?'

(61) Mr Royce. 'There would have to be a deep cutting through high ground to the south-east of Wetherham. This route would be half as long again and would probably cost £8-9 million, compared with £5-6 million for the valley route.'

(62) Mr Spenser. 'That's a lot of money, and I feel doubtful whether this route would be practicable.'

MEETING B

(63) The Chairman. 'Yes, as the valley route has already been criticized for its high cost, there is not much point in suggesting something even more expensive. Your suggestion, Mr Brown, is an ingenious one, but seems scarcely practicable.'

[Comment: The Chairman was at fault in not taking Mr Brown's suggestion seriously and allowing adequate discussion of it, which would have revealed its considerable advantages. As indicated in the comment on item 51, he had already made up his mind that the valley route was the best, and in inviting 'any further comments' he was only going through the motions of consulting other members of the committee. Now he cuts the discussion short.]

MEETING C

(63) The Chairman. 'It might be argued, though, that the extra cost would be worthwhile if it resulted in a route which was much more satisfactory than the other routes which have been proposed. Mr Davis, would you like to comment on whether the extra cost would seem justified?'

(64) Mr Davis. 'Though the total cost of the longer by-pass would be greater, the cost per mile of new road would be slightly less. Or, putting it the other way round, though we should be spending more, we should be getting better value for our money.'

(65) Mr Brown. 'Yes, as I see it, the by-pass following this route, which one might call the "Moors Route", could form the first instalment of a motorway from London to Eastport, which is pretty likely to be needed one day.'

MEETING C

(66) Mr Royce. 'That's a good point. It is a fact that the present main road from Ashstone to Eastport is nowhere more than three-lane in width, and over much of the distance where there are bends there are double

white lines which prohibit overtaking. No section of the road is adequate to carry the traffic now passing along it, let alone the volume of traffic that may be expected in ten years' time. Almost certainly therefore a motorway to Eastport will have to be built within the next ten years. This being so, we should take the long view and prefer a route for the Ashstone by-pass which could, as Mr Brown pointed out, form the first instalment of the motorway, as the valley route, with its semi-circular shape, could not. In the long run, this would save money.'

(67) Mr Greenstick. 'As this route would avoid the good farmland between Loamhurst and Stanbury, it would certainly be better than the valley route.'

(68) Miss Tweedyman. 'I agree that it would do less harm to the amenities of Loamhurst and Stanbury. Also it would keep well clear of Wetherham.'

(69) Miss Ingram. 'Both the valley route and this moors route would be equally satisfactory from the point of view of road safety.'

(70) Mr Magneto. 'Would it be possible for a new garage to be built somewhere along this route?'

(71) Mr Davis. 'Yes, I fancy there would have to be proper service facilities somewhere. This would give a chance also to Mr Andrew to build a new restaurant.'

(72) Mr Jenkins. 'I must admit, I do see the advantages of this route and, despite my own position, I don't feel I can press too hard against the scheme if the rest of you all support it.'

(73) The Chairman. 'Thank you, Mr Jenkins, and thank you, Mr Brown, for what seems a most valuable suggestion. Any other views on this route?'

(74) Mr Goldrib. 'I agree that the moors route proposed by Mr Brown would be a satisfactory route, and, from the long-term point of view, probably the best one. A by-pass is urgently necessary.'

(75) Mr Andrew. 'I agree.'

MEETING B

(64) The Chairman. 'We had better return to the previous alternatives of the valley route and some shorter route and take a vote. Will those in favour of some shorter route please put up their hands?'

Voting. In favour 2 (Mr Greenstick and Miss Tweedyman).

Against 6 (Messrs Davis, Goldrib, Magneto, Spenser and Brown, Miss Ingram).

Abstentions 2 (Messrs Andrew and Jenkins).

MEETING C

(75) The Chairman. 'Then, if I have the feeling of the meeting, we are all agreed that we support the proposal to build an Ashstone by-pass at the earliest possible date. Having considered various alternatives, including the valley route, we consider that the best route would be the longer moors route keeping on the eastern fringe of the Ashstone urban district. It would pass south-east of Stanbury,

(65) The Chairman. 'The proposal for a shorter route has been defeated by 6 votes to 2. Now, we will vote whether or not we favour a by-pass following the commons route. Will those in favour please put up their hands?'

Voting. In favour 6 (Messrs Davis, Goldrib, Magneto, Spenser and Brown, Miss Ingram).

Against 4 (Messrs Andrew, Greenstick and Jenkins, Miss Tweedyman).

(66) The Chairman. 'I personally am in favour of the by-pass, so the motion is carried by 7 votes to 4.'

avoiding the good farmland between Loamhurst and Stanbury, and proceed more or less in a straight line to rejoin the main Eastport road some 5 miles south of Wetherham. This would provide a satisfactory by-pass to Ashstone and also serve as the first instalment of a motorway to Eastport. We consider that the greater cost of this scheme, some £8-9 million, as compared with £5-6 million for the commons route, would be justified and indeed save money in the long run. Are you all agreed on this? Good!'

Final Summing-up by Chairman

Meetings B and C continue as follows:

(76) The Chairman. 'As you know, the next general meeting of the Residents' Association is due to be held on the 18th day of next month. I propose to have the question of an Ashstone by-pass placed on the agenda and to report on behalf of the committee the decisions reached at this meeting. If the general meeting confirms our decisions, we shall then send suitable recommendations in writing to the Ashstone Urban District Council, to the Barsetshire County Council, and to the Ministry of Transport.

Discussion of Interim Measures

Meanwhile, the question remains whether there are any interim measures that we should recommend. Suggestions have been made at this meeting that speed limits might be imposed of 40 m.p.h. on the derestricted stretch of main road, and of 20 or 15 m.p.h. in the centre of Ashstone itself, also that footbridges or subways might be provided to enable pedestrians to cross the main road safely. Of these suggestions the only one that seemed to command general support was the proposal to have a 40 m.p.h. speed limit on the section of the main road between the Odeon and Ashvale roundabouts. It was thought that this should cut accidents without materially slowing down the traffic. Is this agreed? (Other members indicate their assent.) Then, I shall put this proposal also to the general meeting of the Association and, if it is confirmed, the Secretary will write to the Ministry of Transport. Are there any other suggestions?'

(77) Miss Ingram. 'With regard to the position in the centre of Ashstone, pending the construction of a by-pass, I think the general feeling was that some means should be found of making it easier and safer for pedestrians

to cross the main road without obstructing the flow of traffic. One suggestion that occurs to me would be to build island refuges in the centre of each of the four pedestrian crossings, thus making it possible for pedestrians to cross one stage at a time and not, as at present, to wait until the road is clear both ways or to risk getting knocked down or stuck half-way across the road.'

(78) Mr Davis. 'That seems an excellent suggestion. If the main road is not quite wide enough at present to permit island refuges, it could be made wide enough at these four points by taking in a little of the pavement.'

(79) Mr Spenser. 'I agree.'

(80) The Chairman. 'Are we all agreed?' (Other members indicate their assent.) Then I shall put this proposal also to the general meeting of the Association, to be forwarded, if confirmed, to the Ministry of Transport.'

General Comment on Meetings B and C

In contrast with Chairman A, the Chairman in version B intervened to check irrelevancies and to keep the discussion going on what he considered to be the right lines. The meeting therefore covered more ground in less time. The Chairman succeeded in his objective of reaching definite decisions that a by-pass was necessary, and that the valley route was preferable to a shorter route. Each decision, however, was by a majority vote, and the meeting did nothing to reconcile or integrate opposing interests. In his eagerness that the committee should reach some definite decision, the Chairman failed signally in two respects:

(a) He did not lead the committee to reach the best decision available to them. They did not give adequate consideration to Mr Brown's new suggestion at item 54. Had they been encouraged to take this more seriously, they would have come to realize that it was a better solution than the valley route.

(b) He did not enable the committee to reach a unanimous decision. The minority were not convinced that their objections had been answered satisfactorily and so they were not able to acquiesce in the majority view. It must be expected therefore that, though outvoted at this meeting, they would continue to campaign against the majority recommendation.

This meeting was also therefore a failure.

In contrast with Chairman B, the Chairman in version C had in mind the possibility of an 'integrated' solution, not a mere compromise but a fresh proposal that would on balance prove acceptable to everybody. The turning point of the meeting came at item 51, when the Chairman asked members to reflect quietly for a minute or two in case anyone came up with a fresh suggestion. The atmosphere was then favourable for Mr Brown's proposal to command general assent.

The proposal to recommend a by-pass following the longer moors route to the east and south of Stanbury and Wetherham is regarded as the best solution that could be reached by this committee on the information available to them. (Other parties, not represented at the meeting, could conceivably object to this route for other reasons not stated at the meeting.) It would be more expensive than the valley route, and this is why it was not raised in version A and did not find favour in version B.

From the point of view of relieving traffic congestion and reducing road accidents, the moors route would be as good as any other. Compared with the valley route, it would have the following advantages:

(a) It would be a straighter, more direct route and would cost less per mile.

(b) It would do more to meet long-term traffic needs, in that it would serve as the first instalment of a motorway to Eastport.

(c) It would spoil less good farmland and would do less harm to the amenities of Loamhurst and Stanbury.

In view of these substantial advantages, it may be wondered why this route was not suggested at an earlier stage in the history of the Ashstone by-pass controversy. There are two reasons why it may not perhaps be unrealistic to have depicted it as proposed for the first time by Mr Brown at the meeting described in this appendix:

(i) When proposals for an Ashstone by-pass were first mooted before the war, the volume of traffic was much less, the idea of a motorway to Eastport had not been conceived, and a 7½-mile new road following the valley route seemed a sufficiently ambitious project.

(ii) Many proposals that seem sensible and obvious when presented cannot in fact have been obvious until somebody first thought of putting them forward.

ANNEX

Memorandum referred to by Miss Ingram at (4) on page 98

During the first six months of this year the number of road accidents reported as having taken place on the section of main road between the Odeon roundabout and Wetherham was 88. The number of persons injured in these accidents was 62, of whom 11 died. An analysis of these figures according to type of road user is as follows:

	Motorists	Motor-Cyclists	Cyclists	Pedestrians	Total
Injured	13	15	9	25	62
Deaths	2	4	3	2	11

Among the injured cyclists, 7 (3 deaths), and among the injured pedestrians 6 (1 death) were children under eighteen years of age. Thirteen pedestrians (1 death) were injured on the speed limit section of the road in Ashstone, 7 of them (no death) on one or other of the four pedestrian crossings. Nine motor-cyclists (3 deaths) and 6 cyclists (3 deaths) were injured on the derestricted section of the road between the Odeon and Ashvale roundabouts.

INDEX